The Story of North Fork Wine

HISTORICAL PROFILES
AND WINE COUNTRY RECIPES

The Story of North Fork Wine

HISTORICAL PROFILES
AND WINE COUNTRY RECIPES

John Ross

Maple Hill Press

Back cover photo: Dorothy-Dean Thomas

Printed in the United States of America

ISBN 978-0-930545-30-7

ACKNOWLEDGMENTS

I am grateful to the many North Fork people who gave so generously of their time to share their stories with me. I am also thankful for the quiet support of my wife Lois and my children — Sanford, Stewart, and Sarah. They are a constant source of inspiration. My editor, Julie Fleck, and her son Chris at Maple Hill Press are literary professionals who gave me the confidence to embark on a second book. Finally, I must acknowledge the wine itself, which I drink with my dinner almost every night!

– John Ross

FOREWORD

The viticultural appelation, "North Fork of Long Island" was established in 1986. Located in Suffolk County on Eastern Long Island, the area consists of 101,440 acres of land that includes all of the land areas in the Townships of Riverhead, Shelter Island, and Southold. Grape growing and limited wine production on Long Island dates back to the late 1600's, but only since 1973 have there been commercial vineyards almost exclusively planted in vinifera grapes. The total grape acreage on the North Fork is over 3000 acres.

The North Fork is a peninsula surrounded on three sides by major bodies of water — Peconic Bay, the Long Island Sound, and the Atlantic Ocean. It is the water surrounding the North Fork which makes it a distinct grape growing area, rendering it more temperate than many interior places, even on Long Island. The sea breezes moderate the heat in summer and the cold in winter, and limit the number of deep freezes which can damage the vines. The growing season, with a fairly late bud break and a long, warm autumn — along with well drained sandy soil — makes our region competitive with other more established cool-climate viticultural areas around the world.

Long Island's South Fork also has vineyards and its own AVA, "The Hamptons, Long Island" established in 1985. There are currently only three wineries on the South Fork, but they are no less important than their counterparts to the North; thus I have profiled wine people in Bridgehampton and Water Mill.

In one of his columns in *The Suffolk Times*, journalist Troy Gustavson said "Nothing has been more important to the future of this town over the last 30-plus years than the emergence of grape-growing and winemaking as a viable industry." Agriculture on the North Fork has evolved to the point where farmers of earlier generations wouldn't even recognize today's products: micro greens and Asian vegetables; multiple pumpkin varieties; fresh okra, cran-berry beans and garlic; and yes, Merlot, Sauvignon Blanc, and Gewurztraminer.

TABLE OF CONTENTS

PART ONE: Historical Profiles

PART TWO: Wine Country Recipes

PART ONE

HISTORICAL
PROFILES

INTRODUCTION

The story of North Fork wine is just another chapter in the story of the North Fork. Our little peninsula has been a special place for a long time. The native Americans enjoyed the fish and shell-fish, the hunting grounds and the rich vegetation. The English settlers established communities with white frame churches and cleared land for farming. Immigrant families followed, coming from many countries, bringing their culture and establishing a work ethic that still exists today. Long Island ducks and potatoes became famous across America along with our oysters, clams, and lobsters. Commercial and recreational fishermen harvested a plentiful supply of flounder and other fish. Finally, the North Fork has been a vacation retreat for city dwellers since the time of the first railroad in the mid-1800's. The planting of grape vines and the birth of a wine region reflected the rising value of farmland and the suitability of the climate for vineyards. It only needed someone to take the first step.

Interest in wine was growing all over the country. In the late 1960's, wholesale potato farming was declining on the North Fork, so much so that Cornell researchers were looking for alternative crops. The early 1970's saw the beginning of small, high-quality farm wineries in California and upstate New York that challenged the big production wineries such as Gallo, Almaden and Taylor. New York passed the farm winery bill, which provided tax incentives to small scale wineries. In Suffolk County, the newly passed farmland preservation bill allowed farmers to sell development rights to the county, making farmland more affordable to potential winery owners, while other legislation allowed the wineries to hold tastings and sell wine on Sundays.

In 1973, Alex and Louisa Hargrave planted their first wine grapes in Cutchogue. In 1974, Dave Mudd, an Eastern Airlines pilot, planted a small vineyard in Southold. At the time he didn't have a specific plan for it, but he experimented with vinifera varietals and then with grafting them onto native root stocks. He and his son Steve would become a major force as consultants and operators of a vineyard management company.

3

The years 1979 and 1980 were pivotal. Dr. Herodotus Damianos of Stony Brook bought a farm in Peconic and planted it in vinifera grapes, giving birth to our largest and longest lasting winery, Pindar. Ray Blum, an air traffic controller, purchased 30 acres in Cutchogue and planted a vineyard which became Peconic Bay Winery. Lyle Greenfield bought land in Bridgehampton and started Bridgehampton Winery, but the land was poor for grape-growing, and the winery was liquidated in 1992. Peter and Pat Lenz, owners of the South Fork restaurant The Moveable Feast, planted a vineyard in Peconic and called it Lenz Winery. It was sold to Peter and Debbie Carroll in 1988, but retained the Lenz name and has emerged as one of our finest wineries. Kip Bedell, a home winemaker from Garden City, met the Hargraves one summer and worked as a volunteer during harvest. He and his wife Susan purchased a farm in Cutchogue, and Kip went on to become one of our most respected winemakers, establishing Merlot as our dominant grape variety.

This small group of pioneers demonstrated the potential for high quality wine on the East End of Long Island. They have to be given credit for pursuing their dreams, taking the risk, and investing their money in a very difficult business.

They were not the only ones to have an impact, though. The small but growing wine industry attracted many people who would not otherwise have settled here. They came from all over the country and the world. Local people were also trained in the many winery jobs, often becoming professionals in the process. New owners arrived to fuel the expansion of wineries, along with winemakers, vineyard managers, and tasting room people. We also saw the addition of sales representatives, marketers, event planners, and general managers. And we must not forget the field workers and cellar workers. All of these people have contributed to the success of the wineries and have added character to our community. They have enriched the North Fork with their diversity and their love of wine.

The wineries have to be given credit for making our region a destination for many visitors seeking to enjoy its beauty, history and ambiance, and they now sponsor many related activities such as charity events, food and wine dinners, art shows, and live entertainment. The synergy between food and wine has changed the farmstands into centers for specialty produce and many farm-related entertainment activities such as corn mazes, hayrides, pumpkin picking, and corn roasting. The once sleepy restaurants of the North Fork are now becoming culinary destinations, showcasing the best food and wine that our region has to offer. Without the wineries, much of this would not have happened.

Honoring the people who built this industry and those who continue to make it work is the focus of this book. Even after 35 years, this "wine community" is still relatively small and close-knit. As a group, they have changed the North Fork into a food and wine lover's dream and have attracted visitors from all over the country and the world. So many people have contributed to this industry that it has been impossible to mention them all, but I hope the people that I have profiled help you to get to know the whole community a little better. And, finally, I hope that this book encourages you to make the food and wine of the North Fork part of your everyday life.

Long Island Wine — by Siv Codering

You match the liquid in the goblet
to the color of the sky.
"Sauvignon blanc, Chardonnay,"
you say, as if tasting the words.
Then you toast me, take a sip
and lie down on your back
looking up.

The ancient cosmographers
pictured the sky as an inverted bowl
containing all of space,
constant and unchanging,
except for the predictable dance of
the sun, the moon, the fixed and
moving stars.

With a finger, I trace
the hand-stitched edge of a patch
on the old quilt we bought
at a roadside stand, in Indiana,
where we stopped for something
to drink, to while away
the trip.

Some woman, born and buried
not far from James Dean,
cut up her faded dress, the worn
slip, the torn skirt,
and stitched them together
in a predictable pattern: sun, moon,
and stars.

Underneath this quilt,
the earth drinks water infused
with this indescribable light
that tugs at seed, sprout, tendril,
the leaf unfolding pale and chartreuse,
and the clusters ripening
on the vine.

I lie down, feel the faded cloth
soft against my cheek
and the sweet rush of wine
in my veins, as the sky above us
darkens, from Gewurtztraminer
to rose, making water
into wine.

– Presented at Palmer Vineyards, July 9, 1992
as part of the summer poetry series, "Voices on the Vine".

THE LEGACY
OF THE HARGRAVES

Alex and Louisa Hargrave

Alex and Louisa Hargrave were a couple of kids who met at a private party at Harvard University and were married when Louisa was a senior at Smith College and Alex had just graduated from Princeton. Louisa came from Cold Spring Harbor and Alex came from Rochester. They were a very unlikely couple to be planting the first vinifera wine grapes on Long Island in the twentieth century. They had no farming background, nor were they experienced in wine, but sometimes it takes talented people with the confidence of youth to open new frontiers and challenge current ideas.

Alex Hargrave (right) with John Ross

Alex was majoring in political science and seemingly headed to law school. But he hated a pre-law course and enjoyed poetry and languages. Due to the new critical language program adopted during the Vietnam War, Alex began taking Chinese language courses and developed an interest in Asian studies. He went to China after graduation and Louisa transferred to Harvard before they were married in 1968. As young newlyweds, they lived in an apartment in Boston and began learning about food and wine. They read Julia Child and Craig Claiborne (like so many of us) and bought French wine from a local wine store.

While recuperating from a back operation, Alex developed (along with Louisa) an interest in nutrition. They read that eating organ meat or "innards" could be very beneficial to your health.

The only problem was that no one could stand to eat organ meat. So the young couple set out to write a cookbook called "Spare Parts" that would make such things as liver, sweetbreads, tripe, brains, and kidneys both healthy and delicious. The book was never published, but its creation demonstrated their ability to take on challenges that other young people would never consider.

After being frustrated by a refusal by the Chinese government to let them go to China (it was during the cultural revolution), Alex and Louisa packed their Jeep Wagoneer and headed for the West Coast. Ostensibly they were house-sitting for a friend, but they were also investigating the possibilities of wine production. They happened upon Napa Valley during one of the hottest summers on record. Temperatures were over 100 degrees every day. The wine in that sweltering heat did not taste good to them and the notion of buying a vineyard seemed very unwise (they should have talked to Robert Mondavi). They were also unimpressed with Oregon, which seemed to be more interested in clear-cutting forests for lumber than planting vineyards. While standing by Crater Lake, Louisa said "We are out of our element. Let's go back to the East Coast and make red wine from Cabernet Sauvignon grapes like they do in France." One thing they did see in California was a small farm winery with small-scale bottling equipment. It gave them the idea that they could also do this. Wine didn't have to be made factory-style, as at the Taylor Wine company.

Upon returning to the east coast they visited relatives on Long Island, and in November 1972 took a trip to Cutchogue and met John Wickham. The place looked like the garden of eden, and John had grown vinifera table grapes successfully. Alex and Louisa then purchased an old potato farm from the Zuhoski family and planted their first 17 acres of grapes, including Cabernet Sauvignon. Later, their vineyards expanded to 84 acres. The modern Long Island wine industry was born.

At first, the Hargrave farm in Cutchogue was a little like the Woodstock rock concert. It was a happening surrounded by romance and the wonderful feeling that comes from working with the soil. Early employees were part-timers who came to share in the excitement with Alex, Louisa, and younger brother Charlie Hargrave. No one really knew much about farming or about viticulture, but the enthusiasm and willingness to study and learn

8

overcame many obstacles. And the details of farming had to be learned the hard way. Alex bought a new tractor especially designed for vineyard work, but the exhaust pipe blew fumes right in the face of the people planting vines. The salesman took advantage of their inexperience by "forgetting" to tell them about a special attachment. The first wines were released in 1976, and included a Cabernet Rose that was originally going to be a full-bodied Cabernet Sauvignon. It was purchased by many people because of the novelty of Long Island wine, but was thin in texture and light in body with a pale pink color. Because of the impossible expectations by the public and the media, this initial wine was not received as well as they would have liked. The young, idealistic couple were discovering that the business of selling wine lacks some of the romance of making it.

This sometimes-rocky beginning didn't deter the Hargraves from their goal of producing serious wine. By the 1980 vintage their vines had matured, and so had they. Also, a young winemaker from Michigan, Dan Kleck, joined the Hargraves. He would go on to produce some stunning wines for a number of wineries before leaving for the West Coast. In a recent letter, Dan wrote that "the 1980 Hargrave Merlot became a hallmark wine...and that wine is what really got everyone jazzed about the whole Merlot thing for Long Island."

Even more important, the Hargrave wines began to reflect a style that was to become Long Island's signature: vibrant fruit, soft tannins, moderate alcohol content, and crisp acidity. Robert Parker, writing in *The Wine Advocate* of 1984, said "I continue to be amazed by the quality level of certain East Coast wines. Readers in New York should look for the 1982 or 1983 Hargrave Fume Blanc which has a remarkable resemblance to the exceptional white wines of Graves Domaine Chevalier. The 1981 Cabernet Sauvignon is one of the most exciting domestic Cabernets I have tasted in the last year...the expansive perfumed bouquet of cedar, spciy oak, subtle Cabernet weediness, the beautifully textured flavors, and clean, rich finish, suggested the style of one of Bordeaux's finest St. Juliens." By the 1988 vintage, the *Wine Spectator* declared that Long Island wine had "come of age." The courage and persistence of the Hargraves in the early years is sometimes forgotten, but was enormously important.

Castello di Borghese

Marco and Ann Marie Borghese were successful business people from Philadelphia. He had an import business specializing in leather goods and Ann Marie sold expensive jewelry. Marco was considering early retirement in 1998 when he visited a friend on the South Fork of Long Island. They took a ride to the North Fork and visited Hargrave Vineyard. Marco and Ann Marie didn't even know there was a North Fork, but like many others, were captivated by its beauty and ambiance. Marco fell totally in love with the vineyard, the old barns, the tasting room, and the historic, sprawling farmhouse. Later he told Ann Marie that he had bought her a present. She thought it was a bottle of wine. Actually, it was the winery.

Hargrave Vineyards was put up for sale in 1998. Although Alex and Louisa were instrumental in revolutionizing the North Fork and had run a successful business for 25 years, it seems the winery was taking its toll on the family. The land, the winery, and the house were sold to Marco and Ann Marie in the spring of 1999. The Hargraves decided to part ways shortly thereafter. The name of the winery was changed to Castello di Borghese.

Because the Hargraves were the first winery on Long Island and because of the substantial coverage of the event by the

media, the sale to the Borgheses was a major event that was well scrutinized by everyone in the community. Who were these people? An Italian prince from Rome? What is happening to the North Fork? The answer is that Marco Borghese is just one of many very interesting people who have come from all over the world because of our growing wine region. His cultural background and personality have made a great contribution to our community.

Marco was born outside of Florence, Italy in 1943. He is indeed a prince from the famous Borghese family that dates back to the ninth century. Marco went to the University of Rome where he studied engineering. In 1968 he came to New York and went to work for a division of Fiat, buying parts for their airplane division. But at the end of 1969 he moved to Philadelphia, where he became partners with an aquaintance of his father in an importing business. Starting with hair brushes from China (made from pig's hair), they went on to brokering trade in many items from China and elsewhere and when his partner retired, Marco ended up in the leather business.

At first glance, Castello di Borghese looks the same as it always has, with the old potato barn tasting room, the wine-making facility down the lane, and the sprawling old farmhouse. But Ann Marie has transformed the old potato storage area of the barn into a beautiful art gallery where they have had many shows and display beautiful works of art. She focuses on small, upscale events — especially those that involve women. Ann Marie

Marco Borghese and John Ross

teaches people how to become relaxed around wine when in a restaurant or at an event. She gives them confidence in their knowledge of wine. The Borgheses have also moved and rebuilt the tasting room and gift shop so that it can handle more people without changing the ambiance. Over the years, they have encouraged an upscale clientele because of the focus on culture, art, and food. Their wines are well-respected and have won significant awards. Their signature wines are the Sauvignon Blanc which is made from the oldest vines on Long Island, and their Pinot Noir, one of the most difficult grapes to grow year after year. The Burgundy-style Pinot Noir is one of the few made on Long Island. They also produce a rich blended red wine called "Meritage." On the other end of the scale, the Chardonette and Petite Chateau are famous value wines that have been produced by the vineyard for years.

The Hargrave/Borghese winery communicates a sense of history and romance like no other property on the North Fork wine landscape. From the expanded 18th century house where the owners live, to the compound of old buildings where the wine is made, to the converted potato barn tasting room and art gallery, the property reveals the history of our area. The pioneers, the immigrant potato farmers, and now the winemakers all played a role in making the North Fork what it is. It took romantics with a sense of history, like the Hargraves and Borgheses, to preserve this tradition.

Louisa Thomas Hargrave

Louisa helped plant the first vines, made wines that started an industry, and ran a successful winery for over 25 years. She has now resurfaced as an educator and writer, and continues to teach

Louisa Hargrave

people about the science and art of wine, encouraging all of us to make wine (especially local wine) a part of our everyday lives.

After Hargrave Vineyards was sold in 1999, Louisa took a break and attended a wine conference in Australia, and also visited New Zealand before coming home. With a little time to reflect upon the past, she wrote a book,

The Vineyard – the Pleasures and Perils of Creating an American Family Winery (Viking Press, 2003). In this personal and revealing story she tells how she and her husband Alex fulfilled their dream of producing serious Bordeaux-style wine on the North Fork. At this time Louisa also began writing a column for the *Suffolk Times/ News Review Newspapers* called "The Oeno File" which has now been syndicated to the *Southampton and Easthampton Press Newspapers* as well as the NPR radio station, WLIU.

In 2004, Louisa was hired by Stony Brook University to run the Center for Wine, Food, and Culture. As director she has developed a five-year plan to support the viability and sustainability of regional agriculture and introduced wine courses affiliated with WSET – the Wine and Spirits Education Trust. She has also had State legislation passed for wine education and presented three major conferences for our region: Sustaining the Good Life, 2006; Sublime Tastes, 2007; and The Art of Balance, Cool Climate/Maritime Wines in a Global Context, 2008.

Louisa Thomas Hargrave has contributed to our wine community like no one else – first by introducing wine to the North Fork and then by helping us to understand and enjoy it.

The author and Louisa Hargrave

EARLY PIONEERS
WHO SURVIVED THE TEST OF TIME

David Mudd, His Son Steve,
and their Management Company

Dave Mudd has had more impact on the Long Island wine industry than any other person. He and his son Steve planted a one-acre plot of vinifera grapes in a triangle of land across the street from Steve Doroski in Southold in 1974. They shared the same small potted vines that the Hargraves had obtained from California. Dave's curiosity, love of farming, and innovative mind allowed him to experiment and learn at a time when his traditional farming neighbors thought he was crazy. They would ask "What are you going to do with those grapes that you are planting?" And Dave would answer "I have no idea." Well, he may have had no idea, but those early experiments led him to develop a vineyard consulting business that eventually planted 70% of the region's original vineyards and implemented vineyard management techniques that set the learning curve for our area. But who is Dave Mudd and where did he come from?

David Mudd

David was born in 1920 in the farming town of Milwood, Missouri. The town was so poor that it couldn't afford to put two l's in its name. When Dave's father sold their farm they moved to St. Louis, where Dave graduated from Catholic high school in 1938. He went on to St. Louis University and studied accounting. After his first year he took a job with General Motors and continued his education at night, earning his bachelors degree in 1942. But his life changed in 1941 when a high school friend called and asked him to come to a flying course held on Tuesday evenings at the YMCA, really a full-on ground school for pilots. Dave continued on through the primary and secondary phases of this school, but before taking the final phase he was told that he had to join the Air Force Reserve. Shortly after, he was called up to active duty. But instead of assigning him to traditional military service, he was assigned to fly for Eastern Airlines, which had a contract with the military. He was to stay with Eastern from 1942 until 1980.

Early in his flying career, Dave was sent to New York. Initially he lived in Queens, but in 1948 he bought a home in Southold on Jockey Creek. He also became very active in the pilots union known as the Air Line Pilots Association. This was an exciting and important part of his life. Dave felt that the union was good for both the airline and the pilots. Companies that were very bottom-line oriented had to listen to pilots concerned with safey issues. In one incident, Dave felt that a Martin 404 airplane was unsteady when it reached a certain gross weight. He refused to fly it if they loaded it to more than 43,650 lbs. gross weight. When he was told that he might lose his job over it he said, "Fine, but remember, I'm going to be alive."

Dave Mudd's entry into the wine business was due to a fateful visit to the Hargraves. Steve Mudd's father-in-law, John Lademann, was doing electrical work at the Hargraves' and told Dave about it. Dave stopped over and met Alex, inquiring about the new grape plantings. Soon, he had negotiated to buy some of the young potted vines Alex had purchased from California, and the Mudds planted their first experimental acre in 1974. By 1976 they had 26 acres of vines planted along Route 48 in Southold and had graduated from the little potted vines, to purchasing cuttings from UC Davis, to buying a German grafting machine that grafted root stocks of various varieties together. Before long Dave and his son were consulting for many people looking to get into the wine business on Eastern Long Island. The vineyard management company of Mudd Vineyards Ltd. was born. They continued to learn through experience about the soil, the microclimate, and the technology necessary to grow high quality grapes. The Mudds introduced the first mechanical harvester on Long Island. They experimented with drip irrigation, and found that it avoided the problem of water evaporation and guaranteed a successful harvest even in years of drought. They also learned the technology of netting the vines to prevent losing the harvest to the birds. And more recently, they are learning how to prevent deer and even wild turkeys from destroying the crop. After more than 30 years of operation they are still thriving. When asked why they have never got into winemaking

themselves, Dave said that they don't want to compete with their clients, and after Steve gets the harvest in the barn, he needs a little time to go hunting.

I asked Dave, "After all these years of experience, do you still feel that our area is a great place to grow grapes?" and he said, emphatically, "Yes. The long mild fall season is maybe the most important asset, allowing the grapes to slowly ripen with the proper balance of sugar and acidity. The cold, lousy, spring is also an asset in that bud break doesn't come too early, thereby protecting the vines from damage due to spring frost. Finally, the number of days that are over 90 degrees you can count on one hand in a typical year, eliminating problems due to excessive ripening." He feels that our best wines are as good as any in the world.

Finally, what about the impact of the industry on the economy and life of our area? Dave Mudd believes that it is one of the best things that ever could have happened to the North Fork. In the old days, farmers brought in temporary workers only during the harvest because there was no work in the winter. Now, the vineyards maintain workers year-round because of the pruning neccssary to maintain the vineyards. And the other jobs in and around the wine business have brought in many people who would never have been here: winemakers; vineyard managers; tasting room people; event planners; and sales staff — not to mention chefs, B&B's, tour companies and a host of others.

After 35 years the wines of Long Island continue to shine, along with the people who make it happen.

Doctor Damianos and his sons Alexander, Jason, and Pindar

Pindar has always been the biggest winery on Long Island. It is now the oldest winery under continuous family management. Dr. Herodotus Damianos was an early pioneer, and he continues to actively manage his properties even as he turns over many responsibilities to his sons. Pindar Vineyards and Duck Walk Vineyards are now farming about 550 acres of grapes and are producing close to 90,000 cases of wine annually. The Doctor has now been in the wine business for 30 years. From the very beginning, Pindar has attracted more visitors to its tasting room than any other winery. How have they done it?

"The secret to volume in the early days was education. I did some research and found that annual per capita wine consumption in New York state was only 1.7 gallons (this compares to about 17 gallons in Italy). Long Islanders were beer drinkers and when

they went to restaurants they ordered cocktails." So at Pindar they instituted free tours that started in the vineyard, went to the crush pad, into the fermentation tanks, and down into the barrel rooms. The tour guide (who was often Dr. Damianos) would describe each step of the winemaking process, and when they were finally led up the stairs to the tasting room they were able to sample what was being described. Many ended up buying bottles or cases to take home.

Doctor Damianos didn't begin by trying to market a sophisticated vinifera wine. His first wine was a proprietor's blend called "Long Island Winter White." It was a smashing success. This crisp, fruity, cold white wine was made from the Cayuga grape and sold for well under $10 a bottle. A whole generation of Long Islanders were introduced to this wine at Pindar and at stores around the Island. From a production perspective, the Cayuga grape vines produced up to 6 tons per acre of fruit and were ready to harvest after only two

Doctor Damianos

years' growth. Winter White became the first tier of a three-tier system. In the second tier were the varietals such as Merlot, Chardonnay, and Riesling that were first released in the mid 1980's. Then in 1986 the upper tier, Mythology, was released. It was the first Bordeaux-style meritage wine on the North Fork. Mythology came as a result of the work by consultant Dmitri Tchelistcheff, who began working for Pindar in 1985 and stayed until 2005. In addition to Mythology this upper tier included the barrel-fermented Chardonnay, Sunflower, and the 100% Pinot Meuniere sparkling wine called Cuvee Rare.

It wasn't the press coverage about the Hargroves and their vineyard that got Dr. Damianos interested in growing grapes. It went back to a 1969 article in a Cornell Cooperative Extension publication that examined the golden nematode problem in the potato fields. The bug affected 38,000 acres of potatoes, and little could be done except letting the fields lie fallow or planting alternative crops. When the extension people came down from Cornell, they noticed how Bordeaux-like the climate was and asked why no one grew vinifera grapes there (except for John Wickham, a Cornell grad himself). Dr. Damianos became interested in the possibility of a vineyard at that time. In 1979 he bought the 36-acre Krupski farm. The broker who found the farm for sale was Lewis Edson, and Dave Mudd planted his first vines.

Those early years from 1973 until 1990 were exciting times in the Long Island wine industry. Everyone was learning from every source they could find. Our microclimate wasn't exactly the same as other wine growing regions. Many mistakes were made, and often the advisors from upstate Cornell weren't much help. They advised us to use a trellis system that created a large canopy instead of the vertical positioning system now in use. There was also much to be learned about spacing the rows of grapes, and the acidic soil required generous applications of lime to sweeten it up.

Dr. Damianos says that his son Jason provided much insight when he returned from his studies in viticulture at California State University Fresno and later from the University of Bordeaux. Jason has gone on to plant his own vineyard in Jamesport using a strictly Bordeaux model. He will be opening his own winery soon, to be called Jason's Vineyard.

As they have grown older and finished their education, the sons of Dr. Damianos have assumed greater responsibilities at the wineries. Jason is the Director of Winemaking at Pindar and Les Howard is the winemaker. Pindar Damianos, also a graduate of Fresno, is the vineyard manager at Pindar. Alexander Damianos, who has an MBA degree in marketing, is the general manager of Duck Walk and Duck Walk North. The presence of the Damianos wineries on the South and North Fork and the volume of wine that they produce make them extremely important to the future of our region. The Doctor, as he gets older, feels that the Long

Island Wine Council is strong, and the support of state senator Kenneth LaValle has been very beneficial. We need to redefine the definition of a farm and its broad scope of activities before the wineries can grow to their potential. Pindar has been an important player in this journey.

Ray Blum and Peconic Bay Winery

Ray Blum died of pancreatic cancer in 2006 at the young age of 63. He was one of the early, but lesser known, pioneers of the wine industry on Long Island. His wife, Jill, and his daughter Kerri, continue his legacy with Ackerly Pond Vineyards which Ray founded in 1998. Ray planted vines and founded the Peconic Bay Winery in 1979. It was sold to Paul and Ursula Lowerre in 1998 and they have continued the brand while expanding the production and upgrading the facilities.

Ray was a Long Islander who was born in Queens and grew up in Hicksville. He began college at Colorado State and graduated from SUNY Farmingdale with a degree in horticulture. After college he was drafted into the Army and served in Vietnam as a crew member on a medivac helicopter. After discharge he took a job with the phone company when the government conducted a recruiting drive for air traffic controllers. He took up the challenge and was trained in Oklahoma City, returning to work on Long Island for the next 28 years. He retired as an air traffic controller in 1992.

Having read about the Hargraves and their vineyard in Cutchogue, Ray came out to investigate, and wound up buying a 30-acre farm with a house and barns on Route 25 in Cutchogue. He took a one-year leave of absence from his job and planted 17 acres of vines in the spring of 1979. In the next few years, Ray would sell off his own grapes to other wineries and hire himself out to manage other vineyards. He followed the Mudds by purchasing harvesting equipment. He even had a portable bottling line to rent. But by the 1984 vintage he began making his own wine and in 1989 hired Charles Flatt as his winemaker. The early wines of Peconic Bay were good but not the intense, hand crafted wines that they are today. Ray Blum was a very hard-working man who

21

applied his wide area of expertise on a small budget (in a famous incident with fellow owner Kip Bedell, Ray got the nickname "dollar a day Ray" for charging Kip rent on grape lugs during harvest). He lived upstairs in the barn that became the tasting room and the storage area. The wines were made in the surrounding barns on the property.

In 1998, Ray sold the winery and vineyard to the Lowerres. He then went down the road and bought a 16-acre farm on Peconic Lane with a farmhouse and barn. He also married Jill, a retired microbiologist, at this time. They planted 13 acres of new vines and created Ackerly Pond Vineyards. Shortly thereafter, Ray purchased 20 acres of land across the street and, after planting it in vines, sold it to Michael Lynne, the new owner of Bedell Cellars. Finally, Ray Blum bought 65 acres in Southold, of which about 45 acres are planted in vines.

Ray Blum

Perhaps Ray was more well known as a vineyard manager than a winemaker. But what I remember about Ray Blum is that he was everywhere, always helping people out, and always a part of the wine community. In the early days especially, they shared their equipment, their ideas, and their passion for wine. The skills and hard work of Ray Blum were instrumental in the growth of our industry and built the framework for others to follow.

Paul Lowerre is a successful wealth management executive in New York who was looking to get into the wine growing business on the North Fork. By the mid '90's the stage had been set for new investors to enter the picture — the wines were receiving recognition from serious publications and the vines were maturing. More importantly, much had been learned about vineyard management, winemaking, and the marketing of our wines. That was the good news. The bad news was that expenses on all levels were going through the roof. Purchasing a winery became an expensive proposition, and operating the winery successfully an even more expensive challenge. New owners had to be very well-financed and willing to forgo profits for many years. Paul Lowerre was one of this new breed of owner who had a passion for wine but was not planning on doing the work himself. After purchasing Peconic Bay from Ray Blum in 1998, he went on to upgrade every element of the winery, including a group of professionals to operate it.

Matt Gillies was hired as the general manager of Peconic Bay Winery by owner Paul Lowerre. Matt had a vineyard management company, had dabbled in real estate, and had worked in our local wine industry since he was a teenager. With his knowledge of the local wine community, he was able to hire Greg Gove as winemaker and Charlie Hargrave as his vineyard manager. Paul Lowerre backed them by giving them all the resources they needed to produce good wine and to market it to the public. They also developed a friendly, knowledgable tasting room staff, now under the direction of Pascal Zugmeyer, a former sommelier in New York. From the lean founding days of Ray Blum to the present state of the art winery has taken 30 years and a huge commitment of resources. Peconic Bay and other wineries have changed the North Fork into a serious world class wine region and a destination for many visitors.

Kip Bedell

Kip Bedell's motivation to be a pioneer in Long Island's new wine industry wasn't because he wanted to see his name on a label; it wasn't because he was a wealthy investor who wanted to get in on a new business; and it wasn't because he was a wine connoisseur with a 3000-bottle collection of Bordeaux. It was because he was fascinated by the artistry of making wine. His largely self-taught journey to becoming a highly respected and successful winemaker began with a home winemaking kit given to him by his brother in 1971.

John Bedell (nicknamed Kip) was born on Long Island in 1944. He lived in West Hempstead where his family owned a fuel oil

Kip Bedell

business called the Nassau Mutual Fuel Co. Kip graduated from high school and went to Florida to attend Stetson College. It was here that he met Susan Chickering, his future wife. Susan was from South Carolina and came from the family that made the famous Chickering pianos. Kip left Stetson and transferred to Mitchell College in New London, Connecticut where he received an associates degree. After serving in the army for two years in Fort Bragg, North Carolina, he finished his college education at George Washington University, receiving a bachelors degree in business administration in 1970. For the next twenty years, Kip and his wife Susan owned and operated the family fuel business. They settled down in Garden City.

When Kip was in the army he enjoyed going out with friends, and they often drank wine. In those days of the sixties, Taylor Lake Country Red and Matteus Rose were popular. The Matteus bottle made a great candle holder. But this was a time when the whole nation was just beginning to learn about wine. People were realizing that beyond those cheap, sweetened wines made with native grapes there was a whole world of quality wine which Europeans had been drinking for years. Robert Mondavi was part of a revolution in California and Dr. Konstantin Frank was demonstrating that vinifera could be grown on the East coast. And in 1973 Alex and Louisa Hargrave planted vinifera grapes on the North Fork of Long Island.

The wine that Kip made from that home winemaking kit was pretty awful. The raw material was a juice concentrate. But Kip was tenacious and kept making wine in his garage and basement for the next eight years. At the end he was making 200 gallons a year and buying fresh grapes and juice from various sources. He made a stunning Petite Syrah that still exists today. His wine was served to friends and given away as gifts. This hobby was growing into something more serious.

After reading articles about the Hargraves and their vineyard in Cutchogue, Kip came out to meet them in 1974. He also met Dave Mudd, Ray Blum, and Peter Lenz. Kip worked as a volunteer during the harvest at the Hargraves. He was already familiar with the North Fork because his grandfather had a summer cottage in Mattituck. The idea of purchasing land for a vineyard was taking root, but the Bedells thought that it might be just a few acres and not a serious business venture. Ann Wickham, the wife of John Wickham, was a realtor at the time who knew the area and its people well. After attempting to buy a 30-acre piece that later became Ressler Vineyards, they settled on a 50 acre farm that had been in the Davids family for 200 years. It included an old farm house, a barn, and a farm stand on the main road in Cutchogue. They purchased the farm in 1979 and with the help of volunteers planted 7 acres of vinifera grapes in 1980. By 1983 they had planted 19 acres and Bedell Cellars winery was born.

The other early pioneers who had followed the Hargraves were also planting their first vines. Dave Mudd had planted vines in Southold shortly after the Hargraves. He was to become a consultant and vineyard manager for many others. By 1980 Peter and Pat Lenz had planted vines in Peconic; Dr.  Damianos established Pindar, also in Peconic; Lyle Greenfield planted grapes on the South Fork and built Bridgehampton Winery; and

Ray Blum established Peconic Bay Winery in Cutchogue. Much activity was to follow throughout the 1980's.

Susan Bedell was instrumental in the design of the famous label with the two swans, one black and one white on a background of black and white lines. It was simple and instantly recognizable with a local wildlife feel to it. Kip was not initially in favor of calling the winery Bedell Cellars, but his family prevailed. Kip was never a person who sought out the limelight. In fact, his quiet style and seemingly laid back personality presented a vivid contrast to some of his colleagues at the time. Like a chef/owner of a restaurant, Kip became one of the few owner/winemakers who was a hands-on worker in the "back of the house." This focus eventually led to the production of a long line of great wines. His consistency and attention to every aspect of the winemaking process, always learning, helped Kip to develop into the highly respected professional that he is today.

Kip is unusual as a winemaker in that he does not have formal winemaking or viticultural education and he never had the opportunity to work for another winery. When asked what were the critical requirements for the job he stated that a good nose and a good palate are very important. To an extent you are born with these qualities, but you can also develop them by practice and analysis. Kip did take a wine chemistry course in Pennsylvania that helped him with the chemical analysis of wine. During the years when Kip was making wine as a hobby he was developing his nose and palate, learning how to tell when a wine was flawed and how it was changing chemically under different conditions. He can now pick out the subtleties of flavor in a batch of wine before expertly blending it to achieve a desired profile.

Why did Bedell Cellars develop a reputation for its Merlot? And why did Kip Bedell come to be known as "Mr. Merlot"? Kip always favored red wine over white, but when planting those first seven acres in 1980 he planted Chardonnay, Gewurztraminer, Riesling, Merlot, Cabernet Sauvignon, Petite Syrah, and Zinfandel. It was a time of experimentation and watching which varieties took to the local soil and climate the best. Zinfandel and Petite Syrah didn't work well, but Merlot and Cabernet did. Merlot seemed to be more consistent than the others, producing pretty good wine in difficult years and great wine in good years. One of these good years, for all the vineyards on the east end, was 1988. Up to then, Kip had combined the Merlot from the North and South blocks of his vineyard together at harvest. But in 1988 he kept the grapes from the two blocks separate, letting them ferment and develop on their own. He was astonished at how the quality of the south block was much better than the north block. He decided to age and bottle it separately as his first Merlot Reserve. This wine from

Bedell Cellars' Tasting Room

the '88 vintage was highly acclaimed by the press and was instrumental in defining the North Fork as a region of serious Merlot.

By 1990, the Bedells had sold their fuel oil business in Nassau County and committed themselves to the winery as their sole means of support. They sold their house in Garden City and relocated to Cutchogue. They built a very modest tasting room in the front of the barn and hired Cynthia Fuller-Perrine as its manager. Dave Thompson, their vineyard manager, has been with Bedell for 24 years.

The staff was very small at first. but gradually they grew the winery to 30 acres of grapes and production of about 8000 cases a year. By the mid-1990's, Bedell Cellars became profitable as a business and had developed a great reputation for quality wine. Kip sold the winery to Michael Lynne In 2000, but has stayed on as his professional winemaker.

The Pugliese Family

Ralph Pugliese was born into a hard-working restaurant family in Brooklyn. His father was the owner of the Italian American Restaurant, which he opened in 1937, the same year that Ralph was born. Ralph was making wine by the time he was ten years old. It was just a part of the family tradition. He went on to a career in construction where he became the president of the local union.

After reading about the Hargraves and the early years of wine on the North Fork, Ralph came out in 1980 and bought a twelve-

Ralph Pugliese

acre property with a house on it. It was going to be a vacation home, but he and his wife Pat immediately planted a two-acre vineyard. They had purchased the vines from Steve Mudd and were soon to get the bug that lead to commercial winemaking. Their first wine was the 1986 vintage and by 1988 they had made their first sparkling wine, which was to become their signature. Over the years they added more property and vineyards so that they now have 55 acres of property with about 50 acres planted in grapes.

The Puglieses are truly a family winery. Ralph and his wife Pat have worked in it from the beginning and by 1985, Ralph had left his job in the city to devote his time to the winery. Their daughter Domenica is now in charge of the tasting room; their sons Lawrence and Peter share the winemaking and vineyard management duties; and their son Ralph, who is a professional photographer, helps out when needed. They are producing about 7000 cases of wine annually and sell most of them through the tasting room at the winery. They have no distributor or sales staff. They have carved out a niche in the business with their sparkling wines — a Blanc de Noir, a Blanc de Blanc, a Sparkling Merlot, and a slightly sweet sparkler called "Dolce Patricia." In addition, Pat has for years painted the wine bottles for customers, often personalizing them with their names. They also make two Port wines, a white and a red, that are very popular. The Puglieses run a simple family winery that has been around for almost 30 years. They have attracted a wide group of people with their easy going, friendly approach that is never intimidating. The converted potato barn that is the tasting room has been expanded and the duck pond with its grape arbor

Pat Pugliese and Domenica Penny

has become a popular place to picnic. They are a family and a winery that sort of keeps to itself, and Ralph's friendliness and blue collar roots are evident in the wine and ambiance of the winery — and in the loyal following of customers.

Ron Goerler

Having planted a vineyard on Cox Lane in Cutchogue as early as 1982, Ron Goerler is considered one of the early pioneers of our young wine industry. How he ended up with his vineyards in Cutchogue and his winery in Jamesport is somewhat accidental, but it also reflects his view that it is best to keep the two operations separate. Ron comes from a manufacturing background. He owns Crestgood Manufacturing Company in Syosset, a manufacturer of plumbing supplies. Ron considers wine to be a classic example of manufacturing: The grapes are grown in the vineyard; the wine is produced and turned into inventory; and finally the wine is marketed and sold to the consumer. He maintains this separation in order to know the real cost of a bottle of wine from beginning to end. Ron maintains his vineyard operation as a separate business from his winery operation.

The story how he developed Jamesport Vineyards begins with the now defunct North Fork Winery. This winery was founded in 1980 by a group of investors and became one of the industry's earliest casualties, filing for bankruptcy in 1986. Eventually the business was liquidated and Ron Goerler purchased the 4-acre property on Route 25 that included a house and a 150-year-old barn. The Goerlers turned the barn into a modern winery and tasting room and planted a small vineyard surrounding it.

Ron Goerler's interest in wine goes way back to the 1960's when he made wine at his home in Mill Neck. Later, his son Ron Goerler

Ron Goerler

Jr. would become his vineyard manager after going to Cobbleskill Junior College and studying agricultural business. Ron Jr. is now the director of operations at Jamesport Winery, but still heavily involved in the vineyards. For five years the winemaker at Jamesport was Sean Capiaux, a Californian and a graduate of UC Fresno. Sean felt that the climate of Eastern Long Island resembles the Loire Valley in France more than the oft mentioned Bordeaux. Hence, Jamesport has focused on the Sauvignon Blanc and the Cabernet Franc grapes for its signature wines. The Cabernet Franc won the prize for "Best Red Wine" in the prestigious New York Wine Classic, and both wines have won gold medals.

Jamesport Vineyards produces about 7000 cases of wine per year and sells much of it at retail in their tasting room. Their wines are served at Manhattan restaurants such as Aquavit and The Four Seasons, and at many East End restaurants. Ron Goerler has a love of both food and wine, but also enjoys the financial challenge of a true manufacturing business.

THE CORNELL CONNECTION

Bill Sanok

Bill Sanok was the Cornell Cooperative Extension Agent in charge of the agricultural program for Suffolk County in 1973. He was a vegetable specialist who came to the Riverhead office in 1967 with orders to find alternatives to growing potatoes. The potato crop had peaked in 1952 with about 60,000 acres and has diminished ever since. The writing was on the wall that potatoes would not be a viable wholesale commodity in the future. By the late 1960's there was a nationwide increase in the popularity of grape growing for wine production. Professor John Tomkins came from upstate Cornell to Long Island to hold a couple of meetings to encourage grape growing as an alternative to potatoes. Nothing much came of this except for some newspaper articles and extension publications that mentioned the topic. John Wickham of Cutchogue was president of the fruit testing association. He planted a number of different varieties of

Bill Sanok

grapes supplied by the NYS Fruit Testing Association in the early 1960's, and many of these tender varieties performed well, even during the cold winter. But because of religious convictions he didn't want to work with wine grapes.

Professor Tomkins would play a pivotal role in Long Island Wine history when, during Thanksgiving weekend in 1972, he convinced Alex and Louisa Hargrave to drive out to Cutchogue, meet with John Wickham and see his planting of grapes.

Sometime in February, after the Hargraves had purchased the Zuhoski farm on Route 48, Bill Sanok received a call from Alex at Cornell Cooperative Extension in Riverhead. The call was to ask whether the sprout inhibitor that was found in the potato barn would damage the new grape vines that they planned to store there. Bill Sanok went out to Cutchogue and met Alex for the first time. It was Bill's job as an extension agent to make a connection between the farmer with a problem and the researcher who could solve it.

One of those researchers at Cornell was Professor Nelson Shaulis. He was the grape specialist at the time, a viticulturist who specialized in the native Labrusca grapes. He visited the Hargraves several times, as did Dr. Konstantin Frank and Professor Tomkins. The experimental trials that involved the vinifera grapes and the particular problem of growing grapes on former potato fields often created friction between the sometimes arrogant personality of Alex Hargrave, the difficult Dr. Frank, and the academic researchers. Bill Sanok was the ideal person to try and bring them all together. By 1974 Cornell had planted a few vines of its own at the Riverhead experimental farm. And Bill learned how to make wine by attending a demonstration of home winemaking by Cornell Professor Leonard Mattick. In fact, Bill made a very small batch of Gewurztraminer that influenced German-born winery owner Peter Lenz to plant the variety in the new Lenz vineyards.

In the mid-1970's Bill Sanok organized some "twilight meetings" at Hargrave Vineyard and Dave Mudd's office that were open to anyone interested in growing grapes. Early attendees were David Mudd, Kip Bedell, Chris Baiz, Dr. Damianos and others. This group grew into the Long Island Grape Growers Association, the predecessor of the future Long Island Wine Council. Dave Mudd became the first president of this group and went on to become very influential in the fledgling wine business. Back at the research station in Riverhead, Larry Perrine and Rich Olsen-Harbich were getting involved in the experiments with vinifera grape growing and winemaking. The relations between Cornell and the grape growers gradually improved to the point where now they work hand in hand. Alice Wise, who was hired by Bill Sanok in the late 1980's continued this positive interaction.

Bill Sanok feels strongly that the North Fork is a great place to grow vinifera grapes. In the beginning they used the wrong root stocks, set up the wrong spacing and developed the wrong kind of trellising. In addition, they didn't understand the requirements of the soil and, worse yet, the mid-'70s produced some brutal winters. In spite of all that, our industry survived and grew into what it is today. Bill takes a lot of pride in contributing to that success.

Larry Perrine

The story of Larry Perrine, now managing director of Channing Daughters Winery in Bridgehampton, is in many ways the story of Long Island wine. People came from many directions, both geographically and intellectually, to arrive here on Eastern Long Island. Some became owners of vineyards or wineries; some became winemakers, vineyard managers, or technical consultants;

Larry Perrine

and some, like Larry Perrine became all of the above. Larry is an intellectual with a rich educational background. He is also a deep, reflective person. His story began in the suburbs of Los Angeles where he was born in 1951. By the late sixties Larry was a hippie who had attended several colleges before settling down at Cal State Fullerton in Orange County. He received a degree in English in 1973 and met Cynthia Fuller, an English professor who was to become his wife.

But his interests grew in the areas of science and agriculture. It began with a love of plants and evolved into agricultural politics. Larry wanted to help feed the world through knowledge of production and technology. He learned much later that the problem wasn't production capacity but politics. As one of his mentors advised: "Get used to it." This eventually directed him to grape farming and winemaking, things he really enjoyed.

Because of advice from friends and colleagues, Larry ended up at the University of Minnesota in St. Paul. It was the only urban farm campus in the country and he earned a masters degree in soil microbiology. He spent five years in Minnesota going to school, working for the nation's first food co-op, and getting involved in politics with the Democratic Farmers Labor Party. He learned about business management by being the produce buyer for a food co-op called North Country Foods and he learned hands-on farming by helping with the harvest for local sugar beet farmers. He also drank wine, read about wine, and did volunteer work for the first winery in Minnesota, Alexus Bailey Vineyards.

As Larry was getting more involved in political campaigns in Minnesota, his marriage was breaking up because the lifestyle didn't suit his wife. After reading a New York Times article about the renaissance of grape growing in the Finger Lakes of New York, Larry had an inspiration: he and Cynthia would go back to work in agriculture, but this time doing something they liked to do. The logical choice was grapes. He and Cynthia moved to a town in the Finger Lakes in 1980, where Larry went to work for Chateau Esperanza, a local winery in Bluff Point, New York. It had a beautiful setting on Keuka Lake with the hillside vineyards going down to the water. But the winery was a mess. The winemaker was fired just after Larry arrived and the inventory contained a lot of "damaged goods." Larry quickly became the technical person and went to the Geneva Experiment Station of Cornell University for help. It was here that he was recruited by an oenologist to return to graduate school. It was now 1983 and Larry was hired with research money coming from Long Island, where the vineyard experiment was in its early days. Thus began a long and productive relationship with Cornell.

In 1987, *Practical Vineyard & Winery*, a California trade publication, published an article on Long Island's first ten years of winemaking. Larry noticed that the article never mentioned tasting any wine. When Larry questioned this the publisher thought he was crazy to want Long Island wines reviewed by California winemakers. Larry went ahead and set up a blind tasting in California in which they provided six California Chardonnays of their choice and he brought six Long Island Chardonnays. They were all from the 1986 vintage. They were all tasted blind and ranked in order from one to twelve. When the results were revealed, it turned out that the Long Island Chardonnays came in first, second, third, seventh, eithth, and ninth against wines such as Cakebread, Acacia, Chalk Hill, and others. Larry Perrine said, "They were stunned, and I almost pissed my pants!" Long Island wines were on their way.

While still working at Esperanza, Larry received a twenty-ton shipment of vinifera grapes from Long Island. They were assembled by Dave Mudd from half a dozen vineyards and included a mixture of grape varieties that were all harvested at once and shipped upstate. The perception was that being vinifera, they had to be better than the local hybrid grapes being used in the Finger Lakes at the time. Larry learned that nothing could be further from the truth. Mixed, unripe, poorly handled, and shipped a long distance did not make for a quality wine. It was a learning experience.

Larry began to visit Eastern Long Island frequently and talk to the growers. He discovered problems in the vineyard with the leaves turning yellow and unhealthy looking. They suspected a nutrient disorder but could find no literature on the subject. Finally, Larry found German research (on apples) that blamed low soil pH for making "sour soil." And it was discovered that while Long Island's acidic soil was great for potatoes, it was not good for grape vines without the addition of lime. We now see piles of lime at the vineyards. Larry finished his grad program at

Cornell in 1985 and took a job for one year with Dave Mudd. In 1986 Cornell Cooperative Extension created a viticulturalist research position in Riverhead, and Larry Perrine took the job.

In the fall of 1988, Larry was recruited by Dr. Jerry Gristina to become the winemaker and manager at the newly opened Gristina Vineyards. With Peter Gristina as vineyard manager they produced some serious Chardonnay and Merlot. Larry felt the Chardonnay really hit the mark, and the reds were improving by learning how to soften the tannins inherent in their vineyard. They produced about 7000 cases of wine annually. Dr. Gristina and his wife Carol were divorced in 1992, and this had the effect of destroying the growth of the winery. After some management changes Larry finally left in 1994. Dr. Gristina's son Peter left by 1997, and the winery was finally sold to Vince Gallucio.

In the early years Larry was active in the wine council. After the successful Chardonnay conference in 1988, Larry was working on a Merlot conference with the help of Phil Nugent. It was planned for 1990. But also at that time the wine council made a decision to only allow winery owners as members. Larry and others (such as Dan Kleck) were asked to leave. The Merlot conference never happened but what did happen was the first barrel

tasting at Hargrave Vineyard, partially sponsored by Marvin Shanken and *The Wine Spectator*. This occurred in the summer of 1990 and was a huge success. In the fall of 1991 the wine council promoted the first "Windows on Long Island" event at the World Trade Center. Long Island wine was beginning to be noticed.

Larry Perrine had a tough year in 1995 when he had left Gristina and was without a full time job. He did as much consulting as possible to make ends meet. During this period he met Walter Channing, who had planted a vineyard in Bridgehampton, and in 1996 went to work for him at the new Channing Daughters Winery. Larry was joined by former chef turned winemaker Christopher Tracy and his wife Allison. They became partners and have since built the winery into a unique and formidable operation. I think the combination of Chris's background as a chef — where the blending of flavors and the love of food-friendly wines complements Larry's technical expertise and liberal attitudes — has resulted in small quantities of unusual and innovative wines. They grow such varieties as Pinot Grigio, Tocai Friulano, Muscat Ottonel and others. And they utilize wild yeasts and lees contact with white wines to create unique flavors. Batches of a particular wine are often very small and they have developed a cult following through their wine club. About 50% of their production is sold through this club. The newsletter creates an excitement about new releases and the foods that should accompany them.

Formal education, hands-on practical experience, making lots of mistakes, and surviving lots of emotionally charged people problems is how Larry Perrine has grown into one of Long Island's great wine pioneers.

Richard Olsen-Harbich

Thirty years ago there was no set curriculum to become a winemaker on Long Island. Some learned as hobbyists in their garage, some learned as apprentices working for others, and some studied related fields in college. Of these, you could lean toward the chemistry/biology side as did Eric Fry of Lenz, or you could lean toward the farming side as did Rich Olsen-Harbich. Rich graduated with a degree in plant science from Cornell University in 1983. His winemaking has focused on the importance of the vineyard ever since. Rich has also contributed to Cornell's research farm in Baiting Hollow, working closely with Larry Perrine and later, Alice Wise. He is on the viticultural advisory committee and is also the consulting winemaker for the research station.

While still a student at Cornell, Rich got to know some of the people making wine in the Finger Lakes and on Long Island. In 1981 he spent the summer working in the vineyard with Steve

Richard Olsen-Harbich

Mudd, and upstate he got to know Hermann Wiemer. Hermann was asked to consult for Lyle Greenfield, an advertising executive who founded Bridgehampton Winery. Lyle had purchased 34 acres of farmland in Bridgehampton (even though Cornell Extension Agent Bill Sanok had advised against it). Lyle and Rich planted Bridgehampton's vines and by 1982 they had shipped some grapes upstate to Hermann's facility to bottle the first vintage. Rich describes it as a scene out of the wild west. After graduation, Rich became Bridgehampton's first winemaker. He was forced to grow up fast.

By the summer of 1983, Rich was involved in trying to rescue a troubled vineyard that was situated at a low elevation, making drainage difficult. He was also designing and setting up equipment for the harvest in the new Bridgehampton Winery building, Long Island's second, behind Hargrave. With Lyle's advertising and design expertise, the brand was off to a good start. The labels were beautiful and the modern-looking building was a handsome addition to the trendy Hamptons. Rich had to keep up a supply of consistently good wine to an ever-growing market. With all the challenges in their own vineyard, Bridgehampton was only able to supply about 20% of the grapes needed. Rich had to go shopping all over the North Fork for the rest. Thus he became acquainted with Ray Blum, Dave Mudd, Jerry Gristina and many others. Amazingly, by the 1988 vintage Bridgehampton was producing close to 10,000 cases of wine per year. And it was from this vintage that Rich was to make his most famous wine of that era — a 1988 Grand Vintage Chardonnay that was listed by *The Wine Spectator* as one of the top 100 wines in the world. The grapes for that wine came from Gristina's vineyard in Cutchogue. Rich Olsen-Harbich had matured into a wine professional after a long education in the school of hard knocks. Bridgehampton Winery was sold to Peter Carroll of Lenz and then liquated in 1994. The poor vineyard site had proved its undoing.

Rich is on a mission to make great wine. He believes that "the land gives the quality." He also has the conviction, courage and confidence to ignore potentially damaging weather reports and wait until the grapes are ready to harvest. When danger approaches, "don't shoot until the last second" is his motto. The result is that tannins ripen along with the fruit, providing a balanced, complex wine. In addition to a late harvest, Rich likes a long maceration using wild and cultured yeasts. He also uses a process called "saegnee," or bleeding of first run juice, to create a more concentrated wine. He is constantly searching for an interesting wine with its own distinct character. More importantly, Rich is willing to take the risks associated with achieving his goal.

After Bridgehampton Winery was liquidated, Rich worked briefly for the Hargraves, then worked for two years with Jamesport Winery, and did consulting with Larry Perrine before being hired as winemaker and general manager of Raphael Vineyards in 1997. The Petrocelli family built a wine estate resembling the great chateau of Bordeaux. Mr. Petrocelli is on a mission to make great wines in the style of that region. Rich has made that goal a reality. Rich Olsen-Harbich is one of our earliest professional winemakers and he has worked on both the South Fork and the North Fork, experiencing the microclimates of both areas. Using his long experience as a guide, Rich believes the Merlot grape is the signature grape variety of our region and has mastered its nuances. He was instrumental in getting the first official AVA designation of

"Hamptons, Long Island" in 1985, and "North Fork of Long Island" in 1986. In 2000 the third designation "Long Island" was approved. Government regulations state that at least 75% of the wine in a bottle so labeled must be from that AVA (American Viticultural Appelation). These designations provide the buyer with an assurance of origin much like the AOC system in France. In 2005, Rich made a further commitment to the advancement of quality Merlot by founding a group called "The Long Island Merlot Alliance."

While still a student at Cornell, Rich met his future wife Nancy. She was a student at Cornell's School of Human Ecology. She went on to become an educator with Cornell Cooperative Extension in Riverhead and is currently a senior extension agent and respected authority on parenting. The Olsen-Harbich family has two children, Emily and Peter. Rich's laid back style and sincerity along with Nancy's skills as a parent have enabled them to develop over the years in a business that has seen lots of turmoil. They are wine people who have enriched the North Fork with their education and their willingness to share it.

Alice Wise

Alice Wise represents the evolution of what I call the "Cornell Connection" in the wine industry. Her official title is Senior Resource Educator, but her actual job is viticulture specialist for Cornell Cooperative Extension in Suffolk County. She looks like anything but an intellectual and cobweb-laden academic. Alice can be found driving a tractor, trussing up vines, and pulling weeds. She also holds a bachelor's degree in horticulture from the University of Maryland and a masters in viticulture from Cornell. She has been working with the problems of grape growing on Long Island for 20 years and has become an invaluable resource and wealth of information for those involved in the industry.

Libby Tarleton and Alice Wise

The relationship of Cornell to our local wine industry has not always been a happy one. The combination of strong personalities, a brand new wine region, and regional politics created friction along the way. It has been a learning process for everyone. The native and hybrid grapes of upstate New York required a different approach from our vinifera on Long Island. The vinifera in California is grown in a much different climate than that of Long Island. But through the initial guidance of extension supervisor Bill Sanok and the work of Alice's predecessor, Larry Perrine, and the input of Cornellian Rich Olsen-Harbich, the educational bar has been raised. With her quiet, laid back personality, Alice is able to work hand in hand with even the most difficult personalities in the industry and the research labs.

What, exactly, do they do in the area of viticulture at the experimental farm in Baiting Hollow? According to Alice Wise, they have been able to maintain a 2½-acre research vineyard in spite of the enormous expense involved. Over a period of almost 20 years they have studied a wide range of grape varieties and clones. And these are not laboratory clones. They represent a grape variety such as Chardonnay that becomes distinct, with its own flavor profile, over the centuries in a particular region. Alice says that "our Chardonnay trial has allowed the industry to understand the nuances between clones...there are fruit forward high acid CA clones; Dijon clones that are earlier-ripening have a more nutty, minerally, slow-to-develop flavor and a more interesting finish." So researchers will seek out vines that are free of viruses and true to type and then classify them as specific clones. This enables a grower to grow a single clone that matches a stylistic goal or to

grow a variety of clones to create a unique wine. The goal of research has been to define what we could and couldn't do here on Long Island, and to examine the quality of the plant material available. These studies have been enormously helpful to the industry.

As we enter the second generation of wine production, the interest in growing new varietals increases. The public is familiar with Chardonnay, Merlot, and Cabernet. But what about Blaufrankisch, Dornfelder, and Norton? Other new varieties planted include Albarino and Zweigeldt plus two new red viniferas, Segalin and Semebat, both from a French breeding program. These are early ripening reds with tons of color. Alice is growing around 25 varietals to expand the repertoire of successful grapes. Some of these may never end up as individual wines, but they may be the basis for new blends that satisfy specific marketing needs. The research station also studies the entire spectrum of vineyard management from practical ways to reduce herbicide use to new methods of pest control.

Alice Wise works on a small budget with very limited staff. Her only full-time assistant is Libby Tarleton. Libby has a degree in agriculture and is working on a masters in agronomy. She is well-liked by the growers and is able to take full responsibility for projects at the farm. She has been working with Alice for six years.

Cooperative extension is an example of a successful partnership between the county and state, not always an easy relationship. The viticulture advisory committee includes Ursula Massoud, Dave Thompson, Rich Olsen-Harbich, and Larry Perrine. Rich has been our consulting winemaker. Alice feels that their guidance and input has been very valuable. She also appreciates the assistance of the industry through donations, moral support, and actual physical help.

The overall goal is economic development in our region. After all these years, Alice feels that Long Island is one of the most unusual and unique wine growing regions anywhere. We have a sophisticated marketplace nearby that is very knowledgable and demands quality; we have land that is perfectly suited to grow fruits and vegetables of all kinds; and we have a cool climate for grapes that is capable of producing wines of nuance and subtlety. Our knowledge is still very much evolving, but the indications are there for a bright future of delicious wines.

THE WINEMAKERS

The winemaker is to wine what the chef is to food — the central character often playing the starring role As in the chef's profession, entry into the world of winemaking is not difficult in terms of formal requirements. But becoming a master at your craft requires a great palate, basic scientific knowledge about biology and chemistry, enough imagination to visualize the final product, an understanding of farming, and finally the ability to do strenuous, physical labor.

Here on Long Island we have a very diverse group of winemakers who come from many countries and have very different levels of education and experience. This diversity brings some interesting characters to our community and is partially the result of being a new wine-producing region with few established traditions. Some of our best winemakers are virtually self taught, starting with home winemaking kits in their garages. Others began in the vineyard, learning to grow grapes, and eventually moved on to winemaking. And some went through a long, arduous formal education at universities that included internships around the world. What they all seem to have in common is a passion for making wine.

Wine is the fermented juice of grapes. Fermentation is the chemical reaction that changes sugar into alcohol and carbon dioxide. Yeast must be present, along with proper temperature conditions for fermentation to occur. Both sugar and yeast are present in ripe grapes, so that in theory all the winemaker has to do is crush the grapes into a closed container and let nature do the rest. In practice the consummate winemaker has the patience and confidence to know when to leave the wine alone. But there are important control points that require critical decisions if the desired quality and style are going to be achieved: when, exactly, to pick the grapes; whether to use wild or cultured yeast strains, and which ones; whether to allow malolactic fermentation to occur, either naturally or induced; how long to leave the juice on the skins after fermentation; and whether to barrel-ferment the wine or ferment it in stainless steel. Finally, the decisions about aging and the use of oak barrels is critical to the final outcome, as are the final blending decisions.

45

The artistry lies in the ability to detect subtle characteristics in each batch of wine, learning its strengths and weaknesses, and then blending them to achieve a stylistic goal. Each vintage is different due to wide variations in weather throughout the year, so the winemaker can't just work from a standard formula but must approach each vintage as a new adventure. The pressure is intense to make a good wine every time and artistic considerations are often derailed by financial constraints and marketing demands. This makes for a stressful job and is usually reflected in the winemaker's personality. They are always interesting people, sometimes a mixture of the mad scientist and the eccentric artist.

The following winemaker profiles represent "professional winemakers" in the sense that they are hired by winery owners to make their wine. We also have owner/winemakers whose stories are found elsewhere in the book. Some of our professional winemakers do consulting on the side and some of them have vineyards and small production wine labels of their own. Finally, the following profiles do not include all of our region's winemakers, but I hope that these profiles capture the essence of the job and give the reader a glimpse into the world of winemaking.

Dan Kleck

Although Dan Kleck was recruited away from the North Fork over ten years ago by Jess Jackson of the huge Kendall-Jackson Winery, he and a small group of early professional winemakers, including Gary Patzwald and Rich Olsen-Harbich, had a big impact on the future development of Long Island wine. Dan was gifted with an excellent palate; he was full of energy and the willingness to experiment; and he had a very captivating personality. He was hired by Alex Hargrave in 1979 after correctly identifying a wine made from pineapples in Hawaii. More importantly, over the next few years he went on to make some fabulous wines that helped to establish the North Fork as the serious wine region that it has become today. The following letter is from Dan Kleck, now residing in Paso Robles, California:

"My earliest recollection of the Hargrave Vineyard experience back in the late 1970's was that I felt Louisa and Alex somehow

Dan Kleck and Chef John Ross (in hat) at Disney World

belonged to the culinary, political, and social elite, even though they lived a natural life in rural surrounds. Alex was the business brain behind the winery, while Louisa was the worker bee, and she and I, along with Alex's brother Charlie, were the core of the work force. Tak (Jim Takahashi) was our Minister of Culture and Education, and his future wife, Vicky, and the brothers Gillies (Matt and David) rounded out our vineyard crew, along with summer help from Polish neighbor Mike Kaloski's granddaughter, Marilyn Sczewastinowitz. The cellar was fun to work in, and Louisa, Alex, and I all learned a lot together. Louisa had a phenomenal palate. She was an extraordinary cook with a very delicate touch, and she expressed that ethic in winemaking as well. Both the Hargraves had a keen sense for the elegant over the powerful, and we regularly bought 1st-growth Bordeaux or Upper Cru white Burgundies to compare with our own wines, as they could be had for a fraction of today's prices.

"Running a malolactic fermentation on our barrel-fermented Hargrave Chardonnay back in 1980 was my very first foray into such a mystical arena of the winemaking craft. Those early LI winemaking successes were a huge hit with the food media and wine critics, as they were such complementary food wines! Of course, back then one could still walk the Peconic Bay beaches of Cutchogue, New Suffolk, or Southold after a good storm, and pick up enough bay scallops to fill a bucket. Sauteed in butter, those little sweeties were just perfection with our 1980 Hargrave Vineyard Collector Series Chardonnay, with a label reproduction of early American expressionist painter William Merritt Chase's, "The Bayberry Bush." It was engaging to meet all the people we did, back then. Abstract painter Elaine de Kooning (Willem's wife) became a regular at Hargrave parties, and we made those delicious early Long Island Chardonnays to match their work. I especially enjoyed styling a Chardonnay with Roy Lichtenstein's "Brush Stroke II" wrapped around the bottle. We were making fat, buttery Chards back then, and it all somehow seemed to sync together.

"The 1980 Hargrave Merlot became a hallmark wine as well. It was one of the first varietal Merlots that had been made in the state, and one of my first as well. But it was also the first red wine that I thought truly expressed the characteristics of the unique Long Island terroir. We took first place at the International Wine and Food Show in New York City with that Merlot, and that wine is what really got everyone jazzed about the whole Merlot thing for Long Island."

Dan left his job at Hargraves in 1983 and was involved in a number of consulting projects for Bridgehampton, Peconic Bay, Lenz, and Jamesport before becoming the winemaker at Bidwell Winery in 1989 (now Vineyard 48). During this time he made a barrel fermented Sauvignon Blanc that became a benchmark for Long Island. But "Bidwell Vineyard was challenging for me. It presented an opportunity to create a new brand but owner Bob Bidwell was by no means a wine lover...he just seemed to want to put his three boys into jobs, and they were as uninspired and uninspiring as could be. Lackluster sales and low enthusiasm is what led to my exit from their business." In 1991 Dan became the winemaker at Palmer, where he stayed until 1998, winning many awards for Bob Palmer and his growing winery. Dan's willingness to communicate with other winemakers and accept new ideas paved the way for future winemakers who were becoming increasingly professional as the industry grew. Dan was also instrumental in organizing the Bordeaux Symposia of 1988 and 1990. He traveled widely to market Palmer wines including a wine dinner at the Fulton Crab House in Disney World, where I accompanied Dan with the foods of the North Fork. His wines lent an air of creditability to our goal of becoming a nationally recognized wine region.

In those first years of wine production on the North Fork, confronting each task required reinventing the wheel. Choosing varieties of grapes and clones, spacing them in the vineyard, developing a trellis system, and experimenting with different winemaking techniques were just a few of the challenges facing these early pioneers. Dan relates, "Any good fortune I had with winemaking came as a result of an intense curiosity of nature. I loved biology and farming, was comfortable with critters, and growing stuff and getting dirty...it was all part of what motivated my interest in grape growing and winemaking. From rootstock selection to pruning techniques, from canopy management in the vineyards to vat choices, fermentation methods, from cap handling to oak styles...we trialed, we tested, we tasted, we improved upon each step of the process as those early years rolled along." Dan Kleck was a person who thrived in this environment and led the way to the more professional systems that we now have in place.

Dan is now a successful winemaker in Paso Robles in the Central Coast wine region of California. He owns the Silver Stone and Red Horse Ranch labels and consults for Donati Family Vineyard, Orchid Hill Vineyard, Whalebone Vineyard, and Sharp's Hill Vineyard. His wines have won many prestigious awards, just as they did on the East coast. *Wine Enthusiast* magazine gave a 90 rating to his '05 Syrah/Cabernet blend called "Primal." Silver Stone's production of about 2700 cases sells out quickly to a "fiercely loyal clientele." Silver Stone was first made here on the North Fork. Dan was truly a pioneering winemaker here.

Eric Fry and Lenz

"1991 — Eric Fry is mistaken for the Son of God by a Baptist tour group. Religious fanatics flock to Lenz for a viewing. Peter Carroll raises prices by 30%." This outrageous lampoon allegedly written by fellow winemaker Greg Gove says volumes about Eric Fry. In spite of his long shaggy hair, untrimmed beard, and often ragged

49

clothes, he is not the Son of God or even anything close. But he is a unique individual who has had a powerful influence over the evolution of North Fork wines and the driving force behind Lenz Winery for the past twenty years.

The original group of pioneers who followed the Hargraves in the late 1970's and early 1980's were a very diverse group of people: Alex and Louisa were young intellectuals; Dave Mudd was a retired airline pilot; Dr. Damianos was a medical doctor; Peter and Pat Lenz were restaurateurs; Ray Blum was an air traffic controller; and Kip Bedell was a home winemaker. Even though these people and others were learning many lessons about winemaking as they went along, it became clear that experienced, professional help was needed to address growing technical problems and point the fledgling industry in a positive direction. Eric Fry was one of these people.

Eric Fry was born in Columbia City, Indiana, in 1952. He was an excellent high school student with an interest in science. He

and his family had no experience with wine. After graduation Eric worked in a factory which made tractor parts, in order to save money for college. He went to the University of Indiana where he majored in microbiology. After graduation he headed for California and answered a classified ad for a job in the laboratory of Mondavi Winery. The year was 1976 and the Mondavis were having problems with brettanymyces, a bacterial growth in wine. When they met Eric with his degree in microbiology, they immediately offered him a job. He went on to become the lab director at Mondavi over the next three years.

Eric Fry with John Ross

This was an important experience for Eric at a time when Mondavi wines were gaining a world reputation. He was encouraged to enroll in wine courses at UC Davis at the Mondavi's expense. He was also allowed to take a two-month trip to Australia's western wine region and work at the famous Llewellyn Winery in Adelaide.

Even though Eric was becoming an experienced professional in the technical problems of winemaking, he had yet to make wine — and he also had yet to develop the passion for wine that was to come later. In 1981 he quit his job at Mondavi and went to France. He had no job awaiting him, but he did have a good list of contacts. After travelling extensively, he wound up working first in Provence and then in the Cognac region. He learned to speak French and later was to marry a French woman named Dominique who introduced him to the habit of drinking wine with meals.

Returning to California in 1983, Eric took a job with Jordan Winery. He still worked in the lab, but he was also doing work handling the wines in the cellar. He started spending time with the famous wine consultant Andre Tchelistcheff, who suggested that he go to work in New York's Finger Lakes region with fellow countryman Dr. Konstantin Frank. Eric followed the advice and took his first winemaking job at Vinifera Wine Cellars of Hammondsport, owned by Dr. Frank and his son Wally. He learned to make Riesling, Pinot Noir, and even some Cabernet Sauvignon.

By now it was 1988 and the wineries on the East End of Long Island were growing. Peter Carroll had just bought Lenz from its founders, Peter and Pat Lenz. Peter Carroll interviewed many people to become his winemaker but chose Eric because he had a strong point of view. He identified what he thought were the problems at Lenz, and defined how he would fix them. Eric was hired in 1989 and shortly after, in 1990, Sam McCullough was hired as vineyard manager. He too was a professional who was coming into his own. He had a degree in horticulture from the Universtiy of Colorado and had experience with Dave Mudd's vineyard management company. He taught Eric much about the farming side of winemaking and they soon became a formidable team. Now, twenty years later, they are still working closely together. In addition, Tom Morgan had been at Lenz from its inception and continues today as the marketing voice of Lenz. Peter Carroll, a management consultant, left this team intact under the leadership of Eric Fry. Peter has certainly made the important strategic decisions, but always staying in the background. The result has been an unusual consistency and quality in a business that takes years to bear fruit.

Eric Fry has always been an independent character on the North Fork. His beard, mustache, farm overalls, and rugged looks define the man. Politically he is an avowed left wing radical, an atheist, and supporter of many environmental causes. He believes that we live in an overpopulated world and are not doing enough to address the problem. Upon retirement he would like to live in a house where he can produce his own energy, food, and (most likely) wine. But when it comes to winemaking style, Eric is a right-wing conservative. He doesn't like trendy blends, fancy overweight bottles, or exotic labels. He likes varietal character and won't release a wine until it is ready to drink. He has a great deal of patience and confidence in himself, and he has always been eager to share his knowledge with fellow winemakers. Way back in the early 1990's he organized a monthly meeting of winemakers to compare notes and share experiences.

Since becoming the winemaker at Lenz, Eric has made Chardonnay, Gewurtraminer, Merlot, Cabernet Sauvignon, rose, 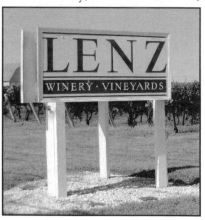 and sparkling wine. Although widely different in style and price, he treats each of his wines equally. His simpler wines are crisp and refreshing, always exhibiting bright fruit. His ageworthy reds and whites are complex wines with deep fruit flavor, soft tannins, and a long finish. All of the wines exhibit an elegance which comes from quality fruit and perfect balance. Eric refers to himself as a "non-interventionist" who interferes with the development of his wines as little as possible, keeping the oxygen out and letting the flavors develop. He uses the term "reductive" to explain this phenomena, and his red wines often have some of that "barnyard" aroma characteristic of Burgundy. He takes special pride in his sparkling wine which rests on the lees (dead yeast) for years in his darkened cellar below the tasting room. When finally disgorged the sparklers emerge with toasty, complex flavors, a creamy texture, and small, long lasting bubbles. But I feel that his finest achievement is the Old Vines Merlot, which is a full-bodied, rich wine that starts softly and grows in complexity and depth until the long finish. It is the embodiment of the term "elegant" and demonstrates the level of quality that we can achieve with the Merlot grape.

Eric's conservative winemaking style, backed up by a well-managed vineyard over a long period of time, has resulted in some of our region's best wine. Eric's persistence has also helped to define a style of wine that is uniquely Long Island, and when asked what differentiates our vineyards from others around the country, Eric will say the long and temperate Fall season.

Russell Hearn and his Custom Crush Facility

Perhaps the most important thing that the wineries have done for the North Fork has been to attract an interesting group of young people from all kinds of places and doing all kinds of jobs. Many have gone on to become professionals in their trade and they have contributed much to the community along the way. Russell Hearn is one of these people. He was born in Singapore and grew up in a small town outside of Perth, Australia. You can't get much further from the North Fork than that.

Since 1991 Russell has been the winemaker at Pellegrini Vineyards. His Australian experience with "new world" wines has given him confidence to use the latest technology available for making wine. He was involved in the design of Pellegrini's winemaking facility. He kept all the winemaking on one level — below ground with a ramp to the crush pad. The barrels are separated from the tank room so that the humidity can be increased as much as necessary.

Russell ferments his red wines in open tanks, which have a pneumatic punch-down device that enables him to give the juice more skin contact, and thus more color and soft tannins added to the wine. He admits that he is an "interventionist" who intervenes when necessary to extract the most from his grapes and to maintain consistency year after year, regardless of what Mother Nature throws at you. His wines are concentrated, with a very firm structure and a chewy texture. Consequently they age very well as the tannins soften and the alcohol fades into the fruit.

While Russell is best known as the winemaker at Pellegrini Vineyards, his greatest contribution might be the development

Russell Hearn

of the Premium Wine Group. From the earliest days local winemakers have acted as consultants to others wishing to produce small quantities of wine. This was usually done in their wineries, utilizing excess capacity. This system works well sometimes but it places a burden on the winery and pressure on the client. In 2000, Russell had the idea to build a custom crush facility that would enable people who owned vineyards (or those who bought grapes) to produce wine without a heavy capital investment in production equipment. He convinced two partners, Mark Lieb and Bernie Sussman, to join him and provide the equity while he operated the business. Now, nine years later, Premium has changed the wine landscape on the North Fork. Many new quality labels such as Schneider Vineyards, Sherwood House, Comtesse Therese, Sparkling Pointe and others are made there, along with the much larger Martha Clara Vineyards wines. Artisanal wines are a fast growing segment of the industry. The vintners market their wines at various small tasting rooms and through their websites. Some use Premium as a starting point to building their own winery production and tasting room facilities. Premium has more than 25 clients in all, producing about 40,000 cases of wine annually. Although Russell and his staff manage the product from start to finish, maintaining strict quality control, they do not make the wines for their clients. This is left to consultant winemakers, mostly experienced professionals already making wine for others on the North Fork. The result has been the production of some very high quality wines that reflect the desires of the owners.

After graduating from high school in Australia, Russell went to a technical college and studied chemistry, earning a diploma in three years. He then went to work for Houghtons Vineyards, a large Australian winery in the Swan Valley from 1978 until 1983. After a short working vacation in the Burgundy region of France, Russell came to the United States, lured here by a girl that he met in New Zealand — his future wife Sue. Sue was from Massachusetts, and Russell took his first job as head winemaker with Commonwealth Vineyards in that state. He stayed there for four years before they moved to Virginia, where Russell became winemaker at Dominion Wine Cellars.

In 1990 he was asked by a friend to do some consulting work on Long Island, at the newly constructed Le Reve Winery. Le Reve was one of the early casualties of our area and shortly went bankrupt. It was at this time in 1991 that Russell was introduced to Bob Pellegini, who was about to build Pellegrini Vineyards. Bob hired Russell and they have had a close relationship ever since. He was able to help in the construction of the winery, working with Bob on buying equipment and designing the layout. Russell was the full time winemaker at Pellegrini for nine years, winning many awards and enhancing its reputation as one of the best wineries on the Island. He is still a consultant for Pellegrini and works closely with Bob and his production winemaker, Tom Drozd.

Russell and his wife Sue, along with another couple, also have a vineyard of their own in Mattituck. It is a 17-acre property on which they grow Bordeaux-style red wine grapes. They will be releasing their own label soon from this artisanal vineyard. They are producing a Merlot and a meritage red blend. Russell's style as a winemaker is an active one where he will intervene in the winemaking process to let the fruit reach its greatest potential. This may involve controlling the malolactic fermentation, heating the tank, or pumping over the must. He has been called a mad chemist by some of his winemaking friends, but he has also earned the respect of the wine community. The quality of his wines are a testament to his skill, and the Premium Wine Group is a testament to his management ability.

Greg Gove

Greg Gove has been a part of the wine community on the North Fork since 1985. He came to the Island with an education in chemistry and biology and with experience as a research assistant to back it up. But in 1985 he had no experience in the world of wine. Learning from the ground up, Greg worked for many years before he was formally given the title of winemaker. But along the way he was making wine, first for the Hargraves, then for Pindar, then for Laurel Lake, and finally for Peconic Bay. Now, at 51 years old, he has won the respect of his colleagues as one the premier winemakers in our region. Since Paul and Ursula Lowerre purchased Peconic Bay from Ray Blum in 1999, Greg has been part of a team that

Greg Gove

includes general manager Matt Gillies and vineyard manager Charlie Hargrave. Not highly visible to the public, Greg has a rich background, a great sense of humor — and perhaps a bit of the mad scientist lurking in the shadows.

Greg was born in the same town as Bob Dylan — Hibbing Minnesota — in 1957. But his family moved frequently because of his dad's job as a civil engineer (his brothers were born in Texas, North Carolina, and New Jersey). The family finally settled in the Hudson River valley, in the town of Tappan. Greg graduated from Tappan Zee high school in 1976. He was interested in studying forestry at Syracuse, but because of financial constraints ended up going to the State University at Cortland. There he enjoyed his organic chemistry class so much that he stayed five years and earned a double degree in environmental chemistry and environmental biology. He graduated from Suny Cortland in 1981.

Upon graduation, Greg applied for a job as research assistant at Columbia University graduate research campus in Palisades, New York. While waiting for that job to materialize he took a summer job as an aide at the county mental health hospital. Perhaps it prepared him for some of the people he was to work with in the wine industry. Finally Greg got the research job and spent the next four years working for Columbia in the organic geochemistry department. It turned out to be a fascinating and productive part of his life. He would go to sea on a 400-foot research vessel for six weeks at a time, traveling as far away as South Africa. Out at sea they analyzed dissolved oxygen in water by taking many samples around the world. They also researched the problems with carbon dioxide in the atmosphere that led to global warming. They also studied how toxic elements were released into the water in the form of acid rain.

But by 1985 Greg was looking for a new challenge. He had read about the fledgling wine industry on Long Island and how they were looking for people with chemistry backgrounds to become winemakers. So he randomly sent his resume to six wineries. The only one to respond was Hargrave Vineyard in Cutchogue. Alex was intrigued by his work with dissolved oxygen in water and wondered how it affected red wine. Alex was also happy that Greg had no wine experience, thus precluding bad habits learned elsewhere. So on August 20, 1985 Greg went to work for the Hargraves. As it turned out this was just before the Island got blasted by Hurricane Gloria, which wiped out much of the harvest and left us with no electricity for a week. But soon they got back to the business of winemaking. According to Greg, Alex was very cerebral and a Francophile. On a day-to-day basis he was as likely to start quoting Jean-Paul Sartre as he was to talk about the technical side of winemaking. He was very good at talking to wine writers like Frank Prial. Louisa would cook up a fantastic bouillabaisse and Alex would quote from the classics. The press loved it.

But there were lots of vineyard problems developing at Hargrave. There were some serious diseases among the vines nescessitating dipping the clippers in a sanitizing solution when pruning. Vineyard management was not Alex's strong point. Since they didn't spread lime to raise the pH of the soil and they didn't hedge their vines, the vines "shut down" early, requiring them to harvest the grapes much earlier than others. They also eschewed irrigation and bird netting, relying instead on Mother Nature and air cannons. By 1988, Greg felt that he had learned much about wines working with the Hargraves, but it was time to move on. On a Sunday in September, Greg told Alex that he wanted to leave but would stay to make sure all the harvest was fermented and racked. The next day Alex accused Greg of pumping gallons of wine into the woods and asked him to resign. Greg responded that after racking the wine off the dead yeast, that is what they always did. Alex didn't believe it. Unfortunately they parted on a bad note.

Greg started working at Pindar immediately after leaving the Hargraves. Dr. Damianos had just bought the former Le Reve Winery in Southampton, turning it into Duck Walk Vineyards. The 1988 harvest was huge and it went on well into November. Greg was hired as the production manager, working with winemaker Bob Henn at Pindar while Mark Friszlowski became winemaker at Duck Walk. They harvested almost 500 tons of grapes that year at Pindar, making many varieties of wine, including *Methode Champenoise* and Port. Greg greatly expanded his horizons during the next nine years and was able to hire some young assistants, including future winemaker Les Howard. Sadly, Bob Henn was developing a serious alcohol problem at the time and it resulted in a deteriorating relationship with Greg. He started getting pretty mean and would try to blame his mistakes on others. Bob was fired in 1997. At this time Dr. Damianos preferred to leave the winemaking title a little vague, stating that the winemaker was Dmitri Tchelistcheff, a wine consultant. But the next week an ad came out stating that the winemaker was Mark Friszolowski, catching Greg by surprise and hurting his feelings. Fortunately, Greg got along fine with Mark. They had even gone to the Soviet Union together, visiting Georgia, on a wine information trip in 1991.

Greg left Pindar in 1997 to take a job building a brand new winery. He said that leaving Pindar was like "stepping off a runaway train." Mike McGoldrick had just bought Laurel Lake Vineyard from Louis San Andreas and wanted a state-of-the art winery. The notion of starting from scratch in a small operation as the head winemaker sounded good to Greg. And it worked pretty well for a while until they started to run into financial problems. Greg quit this job in the spring of 1999. He stayed home to take care of his newborn baby and also worked with Charles Flatt at Pelligrini for a short time.

In 1999, with almost 15 years of winemaking experience under his belt, Greg went to work for the new owners of Peconic Bay Vineyards, Paul and Ursula Lowerre. He teamed up with Charlie Hargrave and they have been working together ever since. He respects the Lowerres as people of integrity who support their staff in a quality operation. Greg likes the fact that they just grow five grape varieties (Riesling, Chardonnay, Merlot, Cabernet Franc, and Cabernet Sauvignon) and produce about 7000 cases of wine per year. Greg is very proud of the condition of the vineyard due to the work of Charlie Hargrave and the overall teamwork at the winery. He seems to have found a home.

Tom Drozd

Tom Drozd is an example of a local North Fork young person with roots in the farming community who grew into the winemaking trade. His grandparents, Joseph and Helen Anderson, owned the farm that is now Jamesport Vineyards. Tom was born in Aquebogue and graduated from Riverhead High School. He attended college at Suffolk Community College, the University of Buffalo, and SUNY Purchase. Tom has a very creative side to him that loves poetry and drama. He has written a substantial amount of poetry and was a close friend of Dan

Tom Drozd

Murray, a published poet and Suffolk English professor. Tom also helped create the "Voices on the Vine' series of poetry readings at Palmer Vineyards in the 1990's. The readings were some of the pioneering events that brought people to the vineyards to enjoy culture amidst the ambiance of the winery.

But it was in 1985, when Tom spent a semester in Italy, that he learned to fall in love with food and wine. In 1987 he took a job at Pindar Vineyards to work in the cellar with winemaker Bob Henn. This apprentice job introduced him to winemaking and in 1989 he moved on to Palmer to work as the assistant winemaker, first under Gary Patzwald and then under Dan Kleck. Tom stayed at Palmer for fifteen years, eventually getting promoted to winemaker after Dan was recruited by Kendall-Jackson in 2000. Dan Kleck sort of set the bar for barrel-fermented Chardonnay on the North Fork, and Gary Patzwald was known for clean, crisp Chardonnay that had not gone through malolactic fermentation. Tom is somewhere in between and likes the fruit-driven style of the North Fork with a subtle use of oak and some malolactic.

In 2006 Tom Drozd left Palmer and became the production winemaker at Pellegrini. Senior winemaker Russell Hearn has been making the strategic decisions along with Bob Pellegrini for many years. Tom is a little out of the public eye at Pellegrini, but very involved in the production of their wines.

Adam Suprenant

The relationship of wine, farming, and food is complex but always present. A good winemaker must understand what goes on in the vineyard and must have a palate that can recognize flavors and aromas that are developed in the wine. This winemaker must also have the skill and judgement to take the raw materials from every vintage and create a palatable wine. Becoming a respected professional involves a long and arduous road of education, experience, and passion. It also takes a person that is eccentric enough to follow this road.

Adam Suprenant is such a person. He grew up in Bronxville, New York in a middle class family. His father managed movie theaters and was an early wine enthusiast going back to the sixties. After high school Adam went to SUNY Morrisville and earned an associate degree. He then transferred to Cornell where he graduated from the School of Agriculture and Life Sciences in 1985. His major was pomology, the science of fruit growing. Adam's family had acquired a small farm and he thought it might play a role in his future. Instead, he took a job working at the newly planted Villa Banfi Vineyard in Old Brookville, Long Island. Fred Frank, the grandson of Dr. Konstantin Frank, was the vineyard manager, and the grapes were made into wine at the

Adam Suprenant

upstate facilities of Vinifera Vineyards. Adam says that this early 1986 job dealing with Long Island vines makes him a "pioneer," but his life was about to take a few more turns before ending up on the North Fork.

As a new college graduate from the suburbs, Adam had a desire to "go to the city." He began by taking a job as an intern with Sherry-Lehman during the holidays. He then became a salesman for a wine distributor, Joseph Victori, that was famous for distributing the "Calvin Cooler." This was popular in what Adam describes as the "bulletproof shops" in the city. In 1988 he took another turn and moved to Brooklyn, becoming a professional waiter and an active member of the Hotel and Restaurant Workers Union — Teamsters Local #6. For four years he worked at places like La Petite Ferme, Cafe Bruxelles, and Regines night club. The pay and benefits were excellent but something in his life was missing.

In 1992 Adam got accepted to the University of California at Davis to pursue a Masters degree in food science and oenology. This is where the road to becoming a winemaker began in earnest. He did internships at the Trefethen Winery, Piper Sonoma, and the famous Lafitte Rothschild in Bordeaux. During the five months in France he also traveled to other wine regions. While finishing his degree, Adam took a job with Franciscan Estate Vineyards in Napa Valley and was on a career path to becoming a California winemaker. But before that could happen he got a call from his dad that a winery on the North Fork of Long Island was looking for a winemaker. The winery was Gristina and the year was 1998. Adam came to Cutchogue and went to work for the troubled winery. He has remained on the North Fork ever since.

Unfortunately, Adam did not get along with Gristina owner Vince Gallucio and they had a mutual parting of the ways. In 2001, he was hired by Bud Koehler to become the winemaker at Osprey's Dominion, where he is today. Adam says that every winemaker must justify his existence through his product. While at Osprey he went through a tough period, especially when Howard Goldberg of the New York Times wrote a disparaging article about their wines. But shortly thereafter, in 2005, the winery won the "winery of the year" award from the NY Wine and Grape Foundation. This prestigious award put Osprey on the quality map and gave some much needed credibility to Adam Suprenant.

Like other winemakers on the North Fork, Adam has become an independent consultant with his own special farm winery license to operate a tasting room and sell wine. He has formed a company called NO FO WineCo and hopes to be marketing his own label while continuing his relationship with Osprey's Dominion. Now 45 years old, Adam has traveled that long road to becoming a respected professional winemaker.

Charles Flatt

Charles Flatt is one of the "characters" in the wine business who is not well known to the public, but is well known for his hard work and colorful personality within the wine community. He has worked as a winemaker and a vineyard manager for a number of wineries on the North Fork since 1989. He is currently vineyard manager for Russell McCall, who grows Pinot Noir and Merlot in Cutchogue.

For Charles, his passion for making wine and working on the land has always exceeded his desire to make money or have an easy life. He started out as a schoolteacher in Pennsylvania before buying a small farm near Bethlehem in 1975. Without formal training he planted the farm in Chardonnay, Riesling, and hybrid grapes. By 1981 he had established Franklin Hill Vineyards, a winery that is still in business today. Due to a divorce and other personal problems, Charles left Pennsylvania and went to Litchfield, Connecticut, wherc he became the winemaker at Haight Vineyards.

And in 1989 he wound up on the North Fork as the winemaker for Ray Blum at Peconic Bay Vineyards. He has workcd on the North Fork ever since.

In 1991 Charles left Peconic Bay and went to work for Gristina Winery, which was making some very good wine after the first vintage was released in 1988, but was in turmoil due the Gristinas' deteriorating relationship and financial problems. During this time, Charles Flatt was instrumental in convincing the Long Island Wine Council to hold the Second Red Wine Sympo-

Charles Flatt

sium — Managing Phenolics, which followed the very successful Bordeaux Symposium of 1988. Charles left Gristina in 1993 and became the production winemaker at Pellegrini Vineyards. There, Charles worked under the direction of Russell Hearn, who had reduced his time at Pellegrini to that of a consultant.

Charles' next move in the ever-changing wine industry on the North Fork was to Palmer in 2000. Tom Drozd was the winemaker and Charles became primarily responsible for the vineyards. And in 2004 Charles landed a job with Split Rock Vineyard Management, a company in Greenport owned by Michael Kontokosta. He has seen the technology, especially in the vineyards, improve and he has enjoyed being part of the region's success. In the past twenty years the wines of Long Island have acquired an identity and reached new plateaus of quality. Employees like Charles Flatt have matured with the industry to become highly skilled professionals who know our soils and climate as never before. But today's high quality wines and growing reputation involved a considerable degree of pain and suffering — and more than a little turmoil among the people doing the work. Charles Flatt will attest to that.

Les Howard

The story of Les Howard and his journey to being the winemaker at Long Island's largest winery is a circular one. Les is a local boy who went to the little one-room schoolhouse in New Suffolk before going off to high school in Mattituck. He graduated in 1993 with the intention of being an auto mechanic, but instead wound up taking a job as a cellar worker with winemaker Bob Henn at Pindar. For the next 12 years he would appren-tice under other wine-makers on the East End and improve his skills. He finally

Les Howard

came back to the place where he began — this time as winemaker at a facility producing 70,000 cases of wine per year, Pindar Vine-yards.

After four years as a "cel-lar rat," Les took his first job as assistant winemaker, this time at Osprey Domin-ion. The winemaker was Bill Skolnik at first and later Peter Silversberg. Bill was an eccentric character who could be very difficult to work for, and Les never forged a good relationship with Peter. But it was a learning expe-rience and after two harvests, Les took a similar job with Roman Roth in Sagaponack on the South Fork. This turned out to be one of Les' best educational opportunities. Roman is a highly skilled and formally educated winemaker from Germany. He had interned in Australia and California before coming to Long Island and opening one of our most sophisticated wineries, Wolffer Estate Vineyards, owned by the late Christian Wolffer. Roman was also a good teacher and an easy man to get along with.

In 2002, after Bedell Cellars had been sold to Michael Lynne, Kip Bedell asked Les if he would like to work as assistant winemaker under him, with the possibility of becoming winemaker when he retired. This too, was a great learning experience, working under one of our most respected winemakers and also being closer to home on the North Fork. Les accepted the job and it went well for a while. But after Trent Pressler came to work for Bedell Cellars as General Manager, it seemed that he wanted to recruit a winemaker with more professional qualifications. Soon he hired John Levenberg from California and Les was left out in the cold. By the 2005 harvest he was working for Ron Goerler at Jamesport Winery as their winemaker. It was a good job, but their operation was small, only producing about 7000 cases of wine annually, and not big enough to hire a support staff.

When Dr. Damianos offered to bring Les back to Pindar with a little bigger paycheck and a larger staff, he took the opportunity and began work in 2007. In the 2008 harvest, Pindar brought in over a thousand tons of grapes that will translate in to about 70,000 cases of wine. Les is hopeful that he will finally emerge as a true professional in this very demanding job.

John Levenberg

John Levenberg is a relative newcomer to the wine community on Long Island. He was recruited in 2005 by winery owner Michael Lynne to help veteran winemaker Kip Bedell develop wines for the next generation of Bedell Cellars. John is a man with an academic background and some intense wine experience around the world. His specialty is coaxing vineyards into delivering grapes that will end up as ultra-premium wines.

John is from the West Hills area of Los Angeles and was a 1989 graduate of Crespi High School, an all-boys Catholic school. He entered the University of California at Davis where he majored in neurophysiology, hoping to eventually become a doctor. In order to help pay his expenses he took a job as a waiter at a small, upscale restaurant called Morrison's Upstairs in Woodland. This student job lasted three years and was John's introduction to wine. They had a good wine list and a friendly owner who spurred the young waiter's interest and allowed him to taste wine and meet the people who made it. When John graduated from Davis and began interviewing medical schools, he talked with one of his mentors, Dr. Alan Dappan, who told him that being a doctor wasn't what it was cracked up to be. This talk made John start thinking about his future and what else he would do if medicine wasn't the answer. And he kept coming back to wine and how much he enjoyed learning about it.

Shortly thereafter he entered the masters program in viticulture and oenology at U.C. Davis. He was encouraged by Professor Anne Noble, inventor of the sensory wheel, who told him that he was qualified to make wine if he had the motivation and desire. While at Davis and after, John completed several internships that taught him the hands-on skills and practical knowledge that he needed. They also instilled in him a passion for wine.

His first internship was with Peter Luthi, winemaker at Trefethen in Napa Valley. He learned about big tonnage Chardonnay and following a precise plan of production. The following harvest he worked with Don Van Staabernan, the winemaker at Artesa in Carneros. Don had just won an award for winemaker of the year. And in 1998, after finishing his course work at Davis, John answered an ad for a job in the Marlborough region of New Zealand. He worked at Te Whare Ra Vineyard for Roger and Christine Smith. This experience was pivotal in that he was in charge of wine-making and ended up rescuing a troubled winery that had good vineyards but mediocre wine. The Gewurztraminer that John produced there won New Zealand's Best of the Harvest Award. John was inspired and on his way.

Upon returning to the California he took a job as assistant winemaker at Cuvaison, a producer of Chardonnay and other wines in Carneros. He was there for three harvests and was settling in as an experienced winemaker. John liked what he was doing, but was not in love with the California style of winemaking that produced big, powerful wines. He was beginning to appreciate the more subtle, food-friendly wines of cool climate growing areas. This interest led him to go to France and take a job at Chateau

Quinault with owner Alan Raynaud. It was another pivotal experience; he got to go off on his own with a project of making a red wine that was fermented in the oak barrels, not the common practice where wine is fermented in stainless steel and transferred to oak afterwards. His wine from this experiment was highly praised and won an award for 3rd best of the vintage. Once again, his passion was spurred. Upon returning to California in 2002 he went to work for Paul Hobbs, an ultra premium winery in Napa. He spent another three harvests working there

John Levenberg

before being recruited to the North Fork by Bedell Cellars owner Michael Lynne. At Bedell, John worked under winemaking pioneeer Kip Bedell and communicated with consultant Pascal Marty. They completely rebuilt the winery into a state-of-the-art facility and produced some very exciting new wines.

John is now a winemaker/consultant with Frank Purita and his wife Claudia at North Fork Wines and Vineyards in Southold. He is specializing in ultra premium wines for a number of clients, including Russell McCall of Cutchogue. The wines of the North Fork are growing in prestige partially because we are attracting some serious winemakers — like John Levenberg.

THE OLD WORLD
MEETS THE NEW WORLD

Wine is a beverage that goes well with food and is often the centerpiece of a special meal. It also flows back through history to the beginning of civilization. People who make wine are part of this culture and carry on the ancient tradition into today's high tech world. Along the way the wine people become a close fraternity with much in common. Technology and education improve, but the fermented juice of grapes remains largely unchanged over the centuries. We refer to "old world" wines, usually meaning those from Italy, France, Germany, Austria, Portugal, and Spain. We refer to "new world" wines from Australia, New Zealand, South Africa, Chile, Argentina, and the United States. On Long Island we are a new "new world" region that is lucky to have the freedom to experiment with grape varieties and methods of winemaking because of the fact that we don't have an established tradition. We are also lucky to have people from all over the wine world

Old World Vineyard, Alsace

69

contribute to our development and share their traditions with us.

Winemakers who came from old world traditions and have settled down on Long Island include Roman Roth from Germany and Gilles Martin from France. Many others have come as consultants. Some have spent the harvest here as interns from European schools of viticuture and oenology.

One of these people, Kurt Janson, came to the North Fork as an intern from the Geisenheim School of Viticulture in Germany. He worked at the Paumanok Winery during the summer and fall of 2001. Kurt is the vintner/manager at his familiy's winery, Schloss

Schloss Janson

Janson, which is located in the village of Bockenheim. His story is particularly interesting to me because he married my daughter Sarah, who has now settled down at the winery with Kurt and their daughter Vivien. Other examples such as this one exist and it is just another way in which the wine industry has affected our lives.

The Mosel River and its tributaries, the Saar and Ruwer, flow into the Rhine at Koblenz. This region has been practicing viticulture since the occupation by the Romans 2000 years ago. The ancient city of Trier was the northernmost capital of the Roman Empire and its gateway, the Porta Nigra, still stands today. The Mosel wine region contains a large concentration of Riesling grapes that grow on the steep slopes of the river. East of the Mosel, along the Rhine, are the Rheingau, Rheinhessen, and Pfalz wine regions. The Rheingau claims to have one of the world's oldest wineries, Schloss Vollrad, and the Rheinhessen is Germany's largest wine region. Germany produces two thirds of the world's Riesling, and the Pfalz produces the most Riesling in Germany. The oldest wine route is the

Deutsche Weinstrasse, running the length of the Pfalz region from the village of Bockenheim to the French border in Alsace.

Bockenheim has been a village with grapes in the region since the year 800. There are 20 wineries in Bockenheim and about 300 hectares (750 acres) of vines surrounding the village. The two largest wineries are Schloss Janson with about 50 hectares and Weingut Sonnenhof with about 40. All of the wineries are family owned and operated. These wineries produce

Kurt and Sarah Janson

a wide variety of wines from many grape varieties. Riesling is most widely grown and the signature grape of the region, but they also grow Silvaner, Grauburgunder, Weissburgunder, Gewurztraminer, and other white varieties. What may come as a surprise to Americans are the red wines that they produce. Spaetburgunder, Dornfelder, Portugieser, and even Merlot represent up to 40% of production for some wineries.

Schloss Janson sits on the edge of Bockenheim at its highest elevation overlooking the village. It used to be a nobleman's castle

John Ross at Schloss Janson

dating back to the 14th century. The ancient wall surrounding the winery is 500 years old, some of the old stone barns are 400 years old, and the present house is about 200 years old. The Janson ancestors were Mennonites with roots in the Netherlands who have been in Bockenheim since 1831. At that time Bockenheim was part of the Bavarian Kingdom before modern-day Germany was formed. They were farmers who grew a variety of crops and raised livestock, in addition to growing about 12 hectares of grapes. They started selling wine commercially about 1900 but it wasn't until 1952 that they became a winery, devoting all their land and energy to the production of wine. Over the years their vineyards increased to the present 50 hectares and their production of wine to about 220,000 bottles per year. They market their wine and deliver it directly to consumers over much of Germany.

The wines of Bockenheim are well made and delicious, but Germans don't seem to take them quite as seriously as we do. They are more of an everyday beverage and their average cost is much lower than those on the North Fork. This is partially explained by the fact that their production costs are somewhat lower since they don't irrigate, they don't use bird netting or deer fences, and they don't hedge and prune as intensively as we do. They not only recycle their bottles, they sanitize and refill them instead of throwing them away. Many local wineries in Germany are entirely run by the families who own them. The lower prices are also due to intense competition from a much larger wine producing region than ours. Germany has over 100,000 hectares of vines, and only a small percentage of German wineries export their wines.

One of the great things about living on the North Fork and experiencing the growth of its wine industry is that we attract a wide group of people from around the country and around the world. In this example, Kurt Janson came as an intern and contributed to our community. Many others have come to stay. And the "old world" influence joins other modern influences to further our education in the world of wine.

The Massoud Family

The Massoud family are the owners and operators of Paumanok Vineyards in Aquebogue, the closest thing we have to a small, European-style family winery on the North Fork. Not only does the family have roots in Europe and the Middle East, but their winery resembles the estate wineries in Germany, France, and Italy. They live in a modest house on the property that sits next to a small tasting room and two barns that contain the winemaking equipment and storage space. Paumanok also resembles Old World wineries in the selection of grape varieties and in the family's intense passion for their wines.

Charles Massoud and his wife Ursula are the founders and chief executives of the winery. Their path to winemaking on the North Fork is circuitous and very interesting. Charles was born in Lebanon and grew up in Beirut. His family always drank wine, but Charles was fascinated by the local silkworm farms that grew mulberry trees to attract silkworm cocoons, which were eventually processed into silk. In 1965, Charles went off to study business at the prestigous Ecole D'Institute Commercial in Paris. In 1967 he made his first trip to the United States by accepting an internship with Chemical Bank in New York. He returned to Paris and graduated the following year, 1968. On the advice of a Lebanese-born American friend whom he had met in New York, Charles applied to the Wharton School of Business in Philadelphia to earn an MBA degree. He graduated from Wharton in 1970 and while there met

The Massoud Family

his future wife Ursula. They were married and Charles accepted a job with IBM. He was then sent to Beirut to work in management of IBM operations there. Soon after, in 1971, he and his wife were transferred to Kuwait, where he would work with IBM for the next seven years. It was during this period in Kuwait that Charles would make his first wine from a home winemaking kit.

Kuwait was a "dry" country in more ways than one. Bringing in alcoholic beverages was illegal, but a home winemaking kit was allowed.

Ursula grew up in Ludwigshafen am Rhein, a small town in the Rheinpfalz wine region of Germany. Her grandparents had a vineyard in the nearby town of Kirweiler. After her mother died, Ursula came to the United States to live with an aunt in New Jersey. She went to school at Chestnut Hill College in Philadelphia where she met Charles. Ursula is steeped in the wine traditions of Germany, including their love of dry Rieslings and other cool climate wines. Because of her connections in Germany, Ursula has sponsored interns at Paumanok from the famous Geisenheim wine school, Germany's equivalent of UC Davis in California. Other interns have worked at Paumanok, including some from France and Spain.

The Massouds came to the United States permanently in 1978 after their stint in Kuwait. Charles worked for IBM in the city and they bought a home in Stamford, Connecticut. In 1979, he read a New York Times article about the newly planted vineyards on the North Fork of Long Island. After reading the article he couldn't

Paumanok Winery

sleep, and soon after came out to see this brand new wine region. In 1983 he bought a farm in Aquebogue and, with the help of Ray Blum, planted 14 acres of Riesling and Chardonnay. By 1993 Charles and Ursula had sold their home in Connecticut and moved to the North Fork. Charles also took early retirement from IBM so that he could devote himself full-time to winemaking. Paumanok now consists of 102 acres of land, 72 of which are planted in eight different varieties of vinifera grapes. From these grapes they are producing about 9000 cases of wine annually, depending on the vintage. The white wines, made from Riesling, Chenin Blanc, Sauvignon Blanc, and Chardonnay, acount for about 60% of their production while the Reds — Cabernet Sauvignon, Cabernet Franc, Petite Verdot, and Merlot — account for the rest.

Charles Massoud has evolved into a serious professional winemaker. Their first vintage was 1989 and the wine was made by Rich Olsen-Harbich, then with Bridgehampton Winery. In the next two vintages Charles made the wine under the guidance of Pellegrini winemaker Russell Hearn. As Charles learned he also passed on his knowledge to his son Kareem who is now his senior winemaker. Kareem's brother Nabeel is the vineyard manager and his brother Salim is in charge of administration. Ursula Massoud is in charge of marketing, but also has a very refined palate that becomes critical when blending the wines. During harvest and other stressful times, the whole family pitches in to do what is necessary. The end result has been one of the highest-quality wineries on the North Fork.

Roman Roth

Roman Roth is a professional winemaker from the "old world" who has formal wine education and has done internships in California and Australia. He has enriched the wine industry of Long Island by giving our wines the credibility and status they deserve. Roman has not only been making wine on Long Island for 17 vintages, he has been one of our most ardent supporters with his presence at dinners, events, and seminars.

Roman was born in 1966 on the edge of the Black Forest in the German town of Rottweil. His father was a cooper and a former winemaker. Roman went to the Weinsberg School of Viticulture where he obtained his masters degree in 1992. While still a student he did internships at the Rosemont Winery in Australia and at Saintsbury Winery in California. Christian Wolffer, a fellow German, recruited Roman to be his winemaker in 1992 when he was just getting started. The beautiful Tuscan-looking building was finished in 1997, and Wolffer Estate Vineyards now has 50 acres of vines surrounding the winery and another 17 acres on

Indian Neck Lane on the North Fork. Richie Pisacano, one of the most highly respected vineyard managers on Long Island, works with Roman as Wolffer's vineyard manager. The winery now produces about 16,000 cases of wine annually.

Roman's German wine background has given him the love of wine with bright fruit character and acidity, but he is also very

Roman Roth

innovative in the way he has used the strengths of the South Fork microclimate to his advantage. With long, slow ripening and careful pruning he achieves elegance and structure in his wines. Chardonnay, which has perhaps gone out of fashion, thrives in Wolffer's vineyards, producing a Burgundian style that is as good as any on the Cote de Beaune. Roman makes Merlot and Cabernet Franc from the vineyards in Sagaponack, but grows his Cabernet Sauvignon on the North Fork. One of his innovations was the production of Verjus, an early-harvested grape juice that is not fermented. This non-alcoholic wine is used by chefs in salads and in sauces accompanying seafood with great results. More recently, Wolffer has produced a rose sparkling wine made from Pinot Noir and Long Island's first Barbera. Roman also took advantage of the troubling end to the 2005 vintage by taking the raisin-like grapes of Cabernet Sauvignon and making an Amorone-style wine from them. The result is an incredibly intense Cabernet that has an alcohol content of almost 16%, hidden in the massive fruit.

Roman has made wine for many others on the North Fork as a consultant winemaker. And since 2001 he has a small production of his own wine, The Grapes of Roth. These handmade wines include a Merlot and a Riesling and are in great demand. They are sold through a private mailing list and to some exclusive restaurants. Roman has made a great contribution to Long Island wine with his professional abilities and his unrelenting energy.

Author's Note: Christian Wolffer, owner of Wolffer Estate Vineyards, passed away on December 31, 2008, while on vacation in Brazil. He was 70 years old. His quest for quality and his enthusiasm for Long Island wine helped establish our region as a producer of world-class wine.

Gilles Martin

Gilles is a highly educated and experienced winemaker from the Old World winemaking region of Champagne. After spending time working in France and on both coasts of the United States, he has settled down in the very New World region of the North Fork. He feels that the French philosophy of winemaking adapted to local conditions has given him perspective that less experienced winemakers don't have.

Gilles was born in Meaux, a small town on the edge of the Champagne region north of Paris. After high school he entered the prestigious Montpelier School of Oenologly where he graduated with a masters degree in 1986. During college he did internships in France and Germany and after graduation he worked in Costieres Nimes, across the Rhone River from Provence. Following the advice of a former professor, Gilles came to the United States in 1988 and took a job as winemaker at Oasis Vineyards in Virginia (coincidentally, Russell Hearn was

Gilles Martin

working at Dominion Cellars nearby). Two years later Gilles moved on to California, taking a job at the prestigious Champagne maker,

Roederer Estates. He stayed in California for six years before briefly returning to France, still working for Roederer.

In 1997 Gilles married Viviane, a French woman who was a professor of linguistics at Rutgers University in New Jersey. His marriage brought him back to the US again, this time as the winemaker for Macari Vineyards on the North Fork. He left Macari in 1999 and began consulting for Martha Clara and others at the Premium Wine Group. Between 2002 and 2007 he worked full time for Martha Clara before returning to consulting at Premium. He has made wine for Sherwood House Vineyards, Bouké Winery, Broadfield Cellars, and Sparkling Pointe Winery. Gilles is especially known for his skill with sparkling wine, and has been involved in the building of Sparkling Pointe's new winery on Route 48, across from Mudd Vineyards.

Gilles Martin is an example of how the custom crush facility at Premium has benefited winemakers and their clients. Small producers can share the same winemaker who works out of a large modern facility. Many economies of scale are enjoyed while preserving the individual character of the wine. Consulting winemakers like Gilles are able to earn a living and make some exciting wines without leaving the premises, and owners are able to market their wines without huge capital expenditures.

MAJOR NEW INVESTMENT ANCHORS THE REGION

Bob and Joyce Pellegrini

The initial group of winery owners were established by 1980. These pioneers included the Hargraves, Dr. Damianos, Peter Lenz, Lyle Greenfield, Kip Bedell and Ray Blum. They were grappling with the many early challenges in and out of the vineyard. But they all went on to make wine, some of it pretty good wine, and they demonstrated to the world that the North Fork was a good place to grow grapes. By 1985 very little wine had actually been released, but the roots of the fledgling industry had been planted and new competition was on the way.

Bob Pellegrini read the article in the New York Times about the Hargraves. He was familiar with the North Fork from visits to a college roommate years before. In 1982 he met Dave Mudd and was invited to a small gathering of what became the Long Island Grape Growers Association. It was this meeting that prompted Bob to start shopping around for land to plant his own vineyard. But his luck at purchasing real estate on the North Fork wasn't good — he encountered many snags in trying to close the deal. Finally, Bob Pellegrini joined Dr. Jerry Gristina as a partner in a 50-acre property on the main road. In 1984 they planted their vines and called it Cutchogue Vineyards. Bob and Jerry had some disagreements, and in 1988 Bob sold his share of the property to Dr. Gristina. It went on to become Gristina Winery. Bob was a little discouraged but, as always, very tenacious. He resumed his search for the perfect vineyard.

Bob's interest in wine grew and he was determined to have his own wine. He even looked at property in Napa and Sonoma near San Francisco, where his son lived. Finally, in 1991 he decided to purchase Island Vineyards from Dick Pfeifle, Charlie Swift and Jim Cassel. It was a 32-acre property on the main road in Cutchogue that had been a vineyard since 1982. It became Pellegrini Vineyards.

Bob Pellegrini was born in the Bronx in 1938. His father was a mason and his mother a seamstress. Bob was inter-

Bob Pellegrini

ested in art early on and attended the high school of art and design. In 1956 he graduated from Christopher Columbus High School and went on to college at SUNY New Paltz. He graduated in 1960 with a degree in art education. At New Paltz he met his future wife Joyce, who was also studying to become a teacher. In later years she would become the business manager of the winery.

Bob's first job was as a junior high school art teacher at the Connetquot school district on Long Island. Soon he went back to college at night and earned his masters degree in fine arts from Pratt Institute in 1962. Bob and Joyce wanted to get away for awhile, so they took a vacation trip to Europe. Just by chance, Bob was offered a job as a civilian employee of the U.S. Army in Heidelberg, Germany. The young couple were to stay there for the next 1½ years. When they returned to the States in 1964 Bob took a job with Time/Life publications and became involved as an art director of the famous cookbook series. But Bob Pellegrini's big break came when he was appointed design director for all publications by the Mexican Olympic Committee for the 1968 Olympics. This became a two year assignment which exposed him to the design world.

After the Olympics, Bob returned to New York and went to work for a corporate design firm which specialized in corporate identity and annual reports. When this firm closed its New York office in 1974, Bob went out on his own and created a design firm that eventually became Pellegrini Associates. This firm is still active today.

By the mid-1970's Bob was developing an interest in wine. He lived in Westchester and joined a wine club, Les Amis Du Vin. At their monthly dinners and tastings he was able to expand his knowledge and experience with quality wine. It was also at this time that news was spreading about the Hargraves opening a winery on Long Island. During the process of building Pellegrini winery and establishing a new brand on Long Island, Bob was able to use his design talents in new ways. His modern, distinctive winery makes a beautiful contribution to the North Fork. With the help of architects Tom Samuels and Nancy Steelman, and winemaker Russell Hearn, Bob created a state-of-the-art facility that has an interior of knotty pine and open space. It stands out with its high tower and creative courtyard, blending into the rural landscape with a look of quality. And his award-winning diecut wine labels with the tiny print make their identity known with just the colors and distinctive shape.

In 1991 Bob Pellegrini hired Australian born winemaker Russell Hearn. He has been their senior winemaker ever since and has had a positive relationship with Bob. Russell's style of winemaking and Bob's vision of what a wine should be are on the same page.

Pellegrini Winery

The result has been a remarkable consistency over the years. Their signature wines are their Bordeaux style reds, including their Vintners Pride series Merlot, Cabernet, and encore. The wines have won many awards and some very good press. They are distributed to the wholesale market by Martin Scott Wines, a premium distributor of small vineyard, estate bottled wines.

Bob Pellegrini has enjoyed the creativity of crafting and marketing his wines. He has also enjoyed the back-to-the-earth feeling of running a farm on the North Fork. It hasn't been an easy process for him, but his determination and tenacity in the face of many obstacles has prevailed, making Pellegrini wines one of the highest quality and consistent wines of our region.

Bob Palmer

Bob Palmer didn't grow up with wine as an important part of his life and he never became a passionate wine collector. But during the years that he commuted to San Francisco as part of his ad agency job, he learned that in San Francisco you must get involved in wine because they won't let you ignore it. He would bring back wine from his trips in the early 1970's to share with his friends. They thought he was a wine expert, so he thought he had better educate himself about wine to back up the perceptions. According to Bob, once you start learning about wine, you never stop. He owned Palmer Vineyards for 25 years and knew much about wine and the people who drink it.

Palmer Vineyards has in many ways written the business plan for a successful winery on the North Fork. Bob understood marketing and how to use it. Back in the 80's all the traffic on the North Fork was on Route 25, what we call the "Main Road." His winery is on Sound Avenue, which at the time was a little-traveled back road (it didn't even have a corn maze). It was so slow that he had to have employees park out front. So Bob put out a sign advertising free hot dogs. All you had to do was buy a glass of wine or a glass of Kool-Aid for children. Wine snobs made fun of him but it worked. Lots and lots of people came, many with their children, and to provide something to do for them, Bob added hayrides through the vineyard. And for the adults he hired a band to play bluegrass music on the deck. This was all years before the current wave of entertainment.

But what about the production of quality wine? Bob Palmer began by hiring Gary Patzwald. Gary produced some excellent early wines, especially reds, before leaving for California. He went on to become executive winemaker at Kendall-Jackson. Gary was replaced by Dan Kleck, who for years was the premier winemaker on Long Island. Dan perfected the art of barrel-fermented Chardonnay at Palmer. He worked for years alongside Tom Drozd, who replaced him when he left for a job in California. Palmer also built a team that included vineyard manager Chris Kelly and tasting room manager Sue Skrezek. During the years of winemaker Dan Kleck, Palmer won more wine medals than anyone. Palmer wines have always

Bob Palmer

been of good quality at a moderate price and they have offered a wide range of style and variety to appeal to a broad market.

Bob Palmer's decision to become a vineyard owner was inspired by a New York Times article about Dave Mudd. Bob called Dave and talked to Cornell Extension agent Bill Sanok before purchasing his property on Sound Avenue. At first he just wanted to grow grapes and sell them to other wineries. But soon he was reminded that in advertising, most agencies were dominated by one big account. "When you wake up in the morning and, while shaving, look into the mirror and wonder if this will be the day when I lose the account?" Bob didn't want to depend on one or two clients to buy his grapes. He reasoned that if he made his own wine it could be distributed to 10,000 clients. His vineyards have grown to 90 acres and his winery produces about 15,000 cases annually.

The marketing expertise of Bob Palmer was a lot more sophisticated than offering free hot dogs. He succeeded in selling his wine to American Airlines, who for many years offered them to first class and business class passengers in transcontinental flights. He was also able to place his wines in Disney World with the Levy Restaurant organization.

The Fulton Crab House has for years featured Palmer wines in the restaurant under a private label. (In 1995 I teamed up with Dan Kleck to prepare an exclusive North Fork wine dinner at the Fulton Crab House. Bob was also able to get us on TV at Universal Studios and to conduct an educational seminar at the Disney Institute). Palmer also has an East Coast sales representative, Tom O'Dea, who markets their wine through distributors from Florida to Buffalo. He works out of North Carolina. Palmer wines are distributed in the New York metro area by Empire.

The winery building and tasting house have changed little over the years. Bob wanted the tasting house to be a separate entity from the winery so that regular customers could bypass the "tour" and come directly to the tasting room. He also wanted it to look like an old-fashioned pub, with a warm and friendly atmosphere. To achieve this, he put in a long wooden bar and a row of antique booths from an old pub. In 2008, he bought two seats from the old Shea Stadium to add a little nostalgia for Mets fans. The covered deck facing the vineyards has always been a popular place for people to enjoy the ambiance.

Author's Note: Sadly, Bob Palmer died of a blood infection on Friday, January 16, 2009, at the age of 74. He was a driving force for our local wine industry and will be sorely missed.

Bill Tyree and Bud Koehler

You often wonder what motivates a successful person to get into the wine business. It is notoriously unprofitable due to its unrelenting expenses, dependence on the weather, the long lead-time between production and sales, and the intense worldwide competition. Those who do get into it often never anticipate how difficult it is. And yet during the 1990's a whole group of successful business people invested in wineries on the North Fork. Bill Tyree

Bud Koehler and Bill Tyree

and Bud Koehler were two of those people. They have known each other since childhood, and both went on to successful careers in construction and real estate. They had been partners before, so teaming up in the development of Osprey's Dominion Winery seemed like a natural thing to do.

Even though Osprey's Dominion didn't make its first vintage until 1991, Bud Koehler had a vineyard since 1983. He was a partner with lawyer Jack Gillies (father of Matt Gillies) in a 24-acre plot near the present winery. In 1985 they added another 16 acres and Bill Tyree got involved by buying out Jack Gillies' share of the land. But they really got involved in 1988 when they purchased the 50 acres of land and the winemaking facility previously owned by Alan Barr of Le Reve fame. When he went bankrupt, Barclay's Bank took over the operation while seeking a buyer. The winery on the South Fork was sold to Dr. Damianos while the vineyard and buildings on the North Fork were sold to Koehler and Tyree. These buildings in Peconic were transformed into Osprey's Dominion Winery in 1990. They now have over 80 acres of grapes planted and are producing about 12,000 cases of wine a year.

Unlike some investor/wine owners, Bud Koehler and Bill Tyree are very much involved in managing the business, especially Bud.

At 79 years old he is working six days a week and guiding every aspect of this business. On top of that, both Bill and Bud are pilots who have flown small planes for many years, including stunt planes and antique biplanes. They both claim that their passion for flying is similar to their passion for wine.

In recent years Osprey's Dominion has been very successful in the use of its sprawling property to attract visitors. On a sunny fall day their lawn will be covered with family picnickers spread out on blankets or sitting at the tables listening to the live band music and drinking wine. The parking lot will have a line of stretch limos waiting to unload at the designated drop-off area. In addition, they are one of the first wineries to be open on weekend evenings, where musical entertainment, dancing lessons, and even book review sessions are taking place. Their 70-foot-long circular bar can accommodate a lot of tasters. About 80% of their production is sold through their tasting room.

Their winemaker Adam Suprenant and vineyard manager Rob Hensen make a wide variety of wines from Sauvignon Blanc and Chardonnay to Cabernet Franc, Merlot, and Cabernet Sauvignon. With 12 acres of Cabernet Sauvignon planted, Bud seems most proud of this varietal. An aged 1995 version of this varietal sells for $99 in the tasting room, but most of their wines are modestly priced from $10 to $35 a bottle. They also make one of the North Fork's few Pinot Noir wines which usually sells out at $35 a bottle.

Bud and Bill seem to enjoy life in general and all of the activity at the winery gives them lots of opportunity to expend their energy. And at 79 years old, it's time to stop stunt flying and do something easy — like running a winery.

The Macari Family Winery

Joe Macari Sr. was born in 1927 and grew up in Corona, Queens. He and his family were part of an Italian immigrant community that was concentrated in that area. There was bocce ball, lots of fresh vegetables and homemade wine. Joe's family ran a candy store that would now be called a bodega. By the time Joe was 18 years old he was helping to run a diner with his uncle. But also at that time he began a part-time sales job with a real estate company, Lewis and Murphy. He left the diner and began working full time in real estate, growing into a job as a business broker. He sold gas stations, bars, grills, and restaurants to many people, including immigrants with whom he had an excellent rapport. He became very successful finding the right person for the right place. As he became more financially stable he began to buy property, much of which was not valuable at the time but would become so later on. He seemed to have an intuitive feel for real estate. After over 60 years he is still with Lewis and Murphy, although his daughter and brother now operate the company.

Joe Macari's introduction to the North Fork came over forty years ago. His sister had just lost her husband and was distraught, with four young children. Joe and his wife Kit had four young children of their own, so they started coming out to the North Fork during summer vacation. It became an annual tradition and they would be joined by the grandparents and others. Joe would commute to work in Queens while the family vacationed. One day in the 1960's he bought a potato farm on the Sound in Mattituck. It had 1400 feet of beach frontage and cost the outlandish sum (at the time) of $3000 an acre. Joe and Kit still own most of that property, about 450 acres. In 1988 they decided to plant

Joe and Kit Macari

some grape vines, partially because their son, Joe Jr., was interested in farming. This vineyard was on Bergen Road.

Also on Bergen Road, but out on Sound Avenue, was the new Mattituck Hills Winery, owned by John Simicich and his family. They had just opened their tasting room and winery in 1991 but soon ran into financial trouble. By 1994 they were forced to declare bankruptcy and the property was auctioned by the bank. Joe Macari purchased it and completely renovated the winery and tasting room. He opened it as Macari Vineyards and Winery in 1998. They now have about 180 acres of land planted in grapes and produce over 15,000 cases of wine annually. Joe Macari Jr. and his wife Alex now operate every aspect of the winery.

The Macari wines have been produced for over 10 years and have developed a reputation for quality. Their inventory starts with a highly regarded Collina 48 that sells for under $10 to a Euro-

pean-style Early Wine that is released shortly after harvest. Their Sauvignon Blanc is a much sought-after varietal along with other wines in the Reserve category. At the upper end they have Bordeaux blends called Bergen Road, Alexander, and Solo Uno that sell from between $42 to $100 a bottle. Joe Jr. supervises the vineyard and the winemaking. He has two winemakers, Paola Valverde from Chile and Helmut Gangl from Austria. The tasting room is elegant with a beautiful deck overlooking the vineyards, but they don't feature a lot of non-wine-related activities and entertainment. They feel that their primary goal is to make good wine. Partially due to the success of the wine club and a growing reputation for quality, their tasting room is very busy.

The Macari family has invested a lot of money in building a state of the art winery and tasting room. Joe Jr. has also been a pioneer in bio-dynamic vineyard management, experimenting with and implementing many procedures to reduce dependence on chemicals in the vineyard. Joe Sr. knows that the incredible operating expenses will eventually be offset by the rising value of the land, and in the meantime the family is very proud of having produced some very good wine. They are also proud to have old friends from the city (and their grown-up grandchildren) come out to enjoy the winery. Joe Macari is still there to greet them.

Bob Entenmann and Martha Clara Vineyards

The Entenmann family, led by Bob's mother Martha Clara, established one of the most famous bakeries in America. The family interest in the business was sold in 1978 and the bakery continued under large corporate ownership. Bob and his family were left with money to invest. One of his investments was to buy property on the North Fork and breed thoroughbred horses. The Big E Farm was established with horse barns, paddocks, and a beautiful mansion. This went very well, but as Bob watched the growing enthusiasm for wine on the East End he reconsidered the use of his land, thinking that he should convert it to vineyards rather than a horse farm. He now has 100 acres of grapes planted and they are some of the most well-cared-for vineyards on the North Fork. Martha Clara Vineyards was established in 1995 and they are now producing about 15,000 cases of wine annually. The tasting room grew out of the old Chickanowitz farm stand that Bob purchased to expand his property. Surrounding barns were remodeled and new ones built to give the winery the look of a farm — which it very much is. They now keep horses to pull the hayride wagons on weekends and goats for the children to see. They also have cows, bison and llamas, in addition to some beautiful peacocks. The idea is to make it all family-

Bob Entenmann

friendly and enjoyable, even for those who can't drink alcohol. Another unusual innovation is that they don't make their wine on the premises, but produce it at the Premium Group custom crush facility located a short distance down the road.

In 1998 Bob's daughter Jackie introduced a design consultant by the name of Bob Kearn to her father. He is an energetic workaholic who became excited with the vision that Bob and Jackie had for their winery. He wound up designing the logo and some early labels along with other marketing ideas. In 2001 he was hired as

Bob Kearn

their general manager. Under the leadership of Bob Kearn and Jackie and the resources of Bob Entenmann, they have created a vineyard and tasting room destination that is always buzzing with activity. They have cooking demonstrations with local and celebrity chefs, art shows, community fund raisers, musical concerts, Octoberfest, and many other events. They also rent space for weddings and provide lots of space for picnicking, watching the animals, riding the wagons — and of course tasting the wine. In some places this would mean chaos, but they have provided the crowds with good parking, large, clean restrooms, and lots of employees to maintain order. Their tasting room and gift shop are organized to handle a lot of people, and they do.

When it comes to the wine, their initial focus was on the whites. They have Chardonnay, Riesling, Gewurztraminer, Vionier, Pinot Grigio, and an upscale blend called Five-O. More recently, they produced a flavored wine called Sabor, aimed at the Latino market but popular with everyone. Their entry-level white is called Glaciers End and their premium reds are a reserve Merlot, a blend called Five-O, and a blend called 6025. They also make a Cabernet Sauvignon and a Syrah. Their *Methode Champenoise* sparkling wine and dessert wines, Ciel and Himmel, are also very successful.

Martha Clara has in some ways created a new definition of what a winery on the East End should be. Or maybe they have just expanded on what has been happening all around. What it has become is an entertainment destination along with being the producer of good wine. To succeed with all this activity requires active management and a lot of adrenalin. At times it looks like a three-ring circus.

THE SMALL ARTISANAL WINERY

Bruce Schneider

When Bruce Schneider and his wife Christiane first joined the wine community on the North Fork in 1994, they were an attractive and very personable young couple, and only 25 years old. They didn't own a vineyard or a winery, and they didn't even live on the North Fork — they lived in Brooklyn. And yet they produced a Cabernet Franc under the Schneider Vineyards label that was to draw high praise from the wine press and more than a little criticism from some wine council members. In actuality, they were merely following the business model of the French negociants that has been used for years in Europe and California, whereby grapes are purchased from high quality vineyards and custom-made into wine at a co-op or other custom crush facility. The Schneiders were pioneers in the growth of small high quality producers on the North Fork that have now become commonplace.

Bruce Schneider

Because Bruce Schneider was young and not well-known on the North Fork does not mean that he was unqualified to make excellent wine. Actually, he is the third generation of a family that has been heavily involved in the wine business. His grandfather, Abe Kass, began as a bootlegger during prohibition in New Jersey and ended up owning a retail wine and liquor store in Elizabeth for 40 years. During that time he became the package store association president and developed many contacts in the busi-ness. Bruce's uncle, Harold Barg, became an executive in Schenley Imports and was involved in bringing Burgundy wines to the United States in the late 1960's. Later, as a high school senior, Bruce would go to France and visit the Vin Expo in Bordeaux with the famous Burgundy producer, Louis Trebuchet. His understanding of quality wine production was forever changed when he worked with Francois Mikulski of the Pierre Boillot house, producers of Volnay Santenot. Bruce's father, Alvin Schneider, was also in the wine business as a broker for Sonoma Vineyards and a distributor of many wines.

In 1991 Bruce took a wine class in New York with Harriet Lem-beck, author of *Grossman's Guide to Wines, Beers, and Spirits*. He also met Carol Gristina of Gristina Vineyards while working in the Democratic Party as a fund raiser for Governor Cuomo. He met his future wife Christiane, who was with the Cuomo press office at the time. This all culminated in a trip to the North Fork to visit the wineries. After talking to people such as Dan Kleck, Larry Perrine, Rich Olsen-Harbich and Kip Bedell, Bruce even-tually hired Sean Capiaux as his consultant winemaker and the wine was made at Premium under the guidance of Russell Hearn. The 1994 Cabernet Franc was his first vintage and it was an instant success. While still a graduate student at Columbia, Bruce entered a contest for a venture capital proposal to plant a vine-yard in Cabernet Franc and make wine. He was awarded the loan and went on to purchase a 21-acre potato farm on Roanoke Ave. in Riverhead. At this time in 1998 he envisioned moving East and becoming a full time winemaker. In fact, he and his wife moved to Stony Brook as a compromise. But the economics were just not there to back up the passion for wine, so they eventually sold the vineyard and reduced the quantity of production. Bruce pur-sued his career in public relations and marketing with RF Binder, where he is now a Senior Managing Director in charge of market-ing beverages around the world.

His Schneider Vineyards label is still very much alive and they are producing some stunning wines including a Cabernet Franc "le bouchet" 2005 that is elegant and resembles the top wines from St. Emilion. The Schneiders have also carved a path for other small producers who are becoming an important part of the North Fork wine community.

Theresa Dilworth

Comtesse Therese is an artisanal winery that has carved out a niche in a crowded wine market, initially with its use of Hungarian Oak, but recently has grown into something more significant. Theresa Dilworth's intelligent and systematic approach to the growing, making, and marketing of her wines on the North Fork is a harbinger of things to come.

Theresa is an attorney who specializes in international tax law. She is currently working for MasterCard. She was a 1985 graduate of Fordham Law School and during her time as a young New York lawyer she had the opportunity to dine at some very good restaurants in the city. This led her to teach herself to cook so she could enjoy fine cuisine at home. And once you get interested in food, quality wine follows close behind. In 1993 Theresa married her Japanese-born husband, Sammy Shimura, and they purchased a piece of property in Mattituck so they could get out

Theresa Dilworth

of the city on weekends. By 1995 they had built a house and had the opportunity to become familiar with the East End wineries. Theresa considered planting a small vineyard on their property, but decided against it because it wasn't ideal for growing grapes. Instead, in 1999, she joined two former business colleagues in the purchase of 40 acres of land in Aquebogue. They now have 20 acres planted in grapes and the 2005 vintage saw their first estate bottled wine. Her husband, a former financial executive in the steel industry, completed a sommelier's course and became passionate about viticulture. Theresa and Sammy went to France with local viticulturist Howard Dickerson, who introduced them to a professor at the University of Bordeaux. From him they met a grad student, Xavier Chone, who became a consultant for them, teaching them about close spacing, low vigor vines, and water stress levels. They have applied this technology to their vines in Aquebogue.

Comtesse Therese wines are made at Premium Wine Group in Mattituck by their consulting winemaker, Bernard Cannac. Initially they purchased grapes from others, and their first vintage was 2001, when they made a Merlot aged in Hungarian oak. In 2004 the '02 Merlot won an award at the New York Wine and Food Classic as the best Merlot in the competition and people began to talk about this new winery. This was followed by a Chardonnay, barrel-fermented in Russian oak, that has also become very popular. And in 2008 they released their first estate-grown wine called First Harvest Merlot, which is aged in French oak.

On the marketing front, Comtesse Therese sells their wines at The Tasting Room, a retail outlet on Peconic Lane in Peconic that sells a number of brands, most of which are made at Premium. The Tasting Room was started by Robin Meredith in 2003. When he sold it in 2006 the new owner had licensing problems and it was closed down. So in July 2006, Theresa Dilworth became the proprietor and now sells nine brands on consignment, in addition to her own Comtesse Therese. But her innovative marketing doesn't stop there. She and her husband have purchased a house on Route 25 in Aquebogue that will be turned into a restaurant called Comtesse Therese Winery Bistro. It is scheduled to open in the spring of 2009. The winery produces about 1100 cases of wine annually and will probably increase that to about 2000 cases as the new vineyard matures.

Christian and Rosamond Baiz

As a seven-year-old boy standing on the beach in late August, gazing out on Peconic Bay, Christian Baiz knew this farm would play an important role in his future. That was 1953 at the farm that his grandparents, Clara and Robert Lang, owned in Southold. They called the farm "The Old Field" because it was once a burial ground for Native Americans centuries ago. It is now called The Old Field Vineyards and is owned and operated by Chris and Ros Baiz. Ros' daughter Perry Weiss is actively involved in every phase of the operation.

Few people know that Chris Baiz planted a small vineyard on this property back in 1974, just one year after Alex Hargrave planted his vines in Cutchogue. His vineyard was less than an acre, but he already was looking for alternative ideas for farming to replace the declining potato and cauliflower crops of the time. Chris bought his vines from the same California source as Hargrave and planted them himself without training or assistance. That original plot included Cabernet Sauvignon, Pinot Noir, Sauvignon Blanc, and semillon. Today they have expanded to 12 acres of grapes that produce about 1200 cases of wine per year. They created Old Field and went commercial in 1997 with the release of their first Pinot Noir. The beautiful farm and its tiny tasting room and winery is like a museum of how things used to be. It is also one of the most beautiful pieces of property on the North Fork.

Christian is the son of an Episcopal priest from Pennsylvania who had a successful parish in Warren, Ohio, where Chris grew up. His maternal grandparents had the farm on the North Fork where Chris and his family would come to visit in the summer. Chris went to Columbia University and graduated in 1970. He went to work as a "roughneck" on offshore drilling rigs for a company called Global Marine and later went to graduate school at Columbia, majoring in mining engineering. He ended up working for a bank

Perry Weiss, Rosamond Baiz, Christian Baiz

as an expert in mining. In 1984 he married Rosamond Phelps and they settled down in Westchester. His trips to the East End continued, and in 1993 his grandmother, Clara Lang, died at the age of 101. After some disputes about the property with his mother's siblings, Chris bought the farm in 1996. He then left his job in the city and moved out to Southold for good. Old Field Vineyard was born.

It's really a story about the use of land, and in this case a beautiful piece of waterfront on the bay with an historic farmhouse and surrounding barns. The passion for making wine and the passion to retain this historic beauty compete with the economic realities of our time: it is very expensive to operate a small winery and follow all the regulations mandated by the community. It is also very difficult to make a profit from a small production winery. The Baiz family has developed a wine club and attracts visitors to enjoy the historic beauty. They also make good wine with the consulting help of Eric Fry, winemaker at Lenz. It's a romantic vision that struggles in a very practical world.

The Old Field Vineyards tasting room

The Tasting Room in Peconic:
an outlet for wines without a winery

The Tasting Room, a small structure on Peconic Lane, was a natural outgrowth of the Premium custom crush facility in Mattituck. People have always been able to consult with a winemaker at one of the existing wineries and perhaps have a custom wine made there using excess capacity of the winery. But Russell Hearn's Premium Wine Group creates an opportunity for many people to become vintners without having to buy equipment or, in some cases, to own a vineyard. Robin Meredith opened The Tasting Room in 2003 and it was taken over by Theresa Dilworth in 2006. Charlie Lazarou is now her manager, and he over-sees ten brands being sold on consignment.

Some of the brands being sold at the Tasting Room represent owners who are still getting established and will soon have their own tasting facilities. Others are artisanal wines made in small quantities that need a central location to display and sell their wines. In this high tech

Charlie Lazarou

age of communication, every brand seems to have a website from which you can order wine and learn about the producer. The Tasting Room is a tangible outlet that can augment the website.

In 2008, the following wines were being sold at the Tasting Room:

Bouké Winery, owned by Lisa Donneson
Bridge Vineyards, owned by Greg Sandor and Paul Wegimont
Brooklyn Oenology Winery
Christiano Family Vineyards
Comtesse Therese Vineyards, owned by Theresa Dilworth
Medolla Vineyards
On A Bay Vineyards, owned by the Anderson family
Sherwood House Vineyards, owned by Charles and Barbara Smithen
Schneider Vineyards, owned by Bruce Schneider
Sparkling Pointe Winery, owned by Tom and Cynthia Rosicki

As our region develops and enters the second generation of winemaking, the variety of wines, and the people who produce them continues to grow. It just shows how a 750ml bottle of fermented grape juice can take on such great proportions and stimulate the passion of so many people.

The Tasting Room

Sal and Maryann Diliberto

There are a small group of winemakers on the North Fork who started by making wine at home. It usually starts with a winemaking kit and a book of instructions. The crushed grapes, the smell of the yeast as it ferments the juice, and the joy of creation provide a satisfaction that has to be experienced to be appreciated. Sal Diliberto is an attorney from Queens who enjoys every facet of winemaking. He and his wife Maryann also enjoy the people who drink wine.

It began for Sal at the Ridgewood Beer and Wine Store in Maspeth. The year was 1985. Sal made the wine from California grapes purchased at a Brooklyn market which he crushed on his patio and piped to his basement cellar for aging. He loved the process of making wine and soon discovered that he could buy better grapes (and much fresher ones) on the North Fork. He began purchasing grapes and seeking advice from Ray Blum at Peconic Bay Vineyards.

Maryann and Sal Diliberto

He would load them into his station wagon and return to Queens. On one trip he bought 1000 pounds of grapes, crammed them into the station wagon, and headed for home. At the traffic circle in Riverhead, one of his tires blew out. The home wine production was clearly getting out of hand and it was time to move to the North Fork.

In 1991 they bought a home on a two-acre plot of land in Jamesport. They added two more acres and leased another two so that they could plant four acres of grapes. The small vineyard contains Sauvignon Blanc, Chardonnay, Merlot, and Cabernet Sauvignon. 2001 was the first vintage for the new Diliberto Winery. After some help with the vines from Howard Dickerson, Sal became the winemaker, vineyard manager, and CEO. All of his home prac-

tice paid off because his wines were an immediate success. He won gold medals in the NY Wine and Food Classic in 2004 and his '03 Merlot won the "Best Merlot" in the '05 competition.

In 2007 the Dilibertos opened their tasting room in a small building next to the vineyard that looks like an outdoor piazza in Italy. The walls are covered with murals and there are pic-

tures of nudes behind the tiny tasting bar. The room has small tables and chairs like those in a cafe where people sit to taste the wines. Italian opera music or on busy weekends live musicians contribute to the ambiance. Sal and Maryann enjoy the sociability of their tasting room and the people who come there. With the addition of a wine club, they have developed a following who come and bring their friends. They are now producing around 1000 cases per year, sold almost exclusively from the tasting room. And on a sunny afternoon in the summer, their back yard is full of people happily drinking wine.

Michael and Paula Croteaux

As the Long Island wine industry enters its second generation, we are seeing the beginnings of specialization. Winery growth at present seems to be concentrated on small producers who are located off the beaten path and offer the customer quality wine with a personal attachment. Eschewing the crowds at the long tasting bars of some wineries, people are discovering places where the

Michael and Paula Croteaux

owner pours your wine and literally invites you into his or her house.

Croteaux Vineyards is located on an historic farm property previously owned by the Howell family going back to the 18th century. It is on South Harbor Lane in Southold and has ten acres of vines surrounding an old farmhouse and even older barns. Michael and Paula live in the farmhouse, where she conducts a very popular cooking school. The tiny tasting barn opens onto a beautiful patio that overlooks the exposed beams of an ancient wooden barn. To visit this winery is, by design, a very personal experience.

Croteaux Vineyards produces only rose. Why? Michael explains that it is a "lifestyle" wine. We are a summer resort area located near beautiful ocean beaches and picturesque bays. As in the Provence region of France, rose is the perfect wine to drink during the warm months and for the casual occasions that are so popular. Croteaux's slogan is "Rose on Purpose!" They make their rose exclusively from the Merlot grape, purposely using three different clones to create distinctive individual character. One of the clones is barrel-fermented and undergoes malalactic fermentation, unusual for a rose anywhere. The Merlot grape was chosen because it thrives on the North Fork and, because it's a rose, can be harvested a little earlier than tradional red wine grapes. Croteaux's first vintage was 2006 and their tasting room opened in 2007. They are producing about 1000 cases of wine annually. They also

Old Barn at Croteaux

sell some of their other grapes (Sauvignon Blanc and Cabernet Franc) to other wineries. Croteaux's wines are made by Rich Olsen-Harbich at Raphael.

Although Croteaux only opened in 2007, Paula and Michael have been around the local wine industry a long time. The former Paula Skwara was born on the North Fork and graduated from Southold High School in 1974. Michael owns a graphic design firm in Manhattan that, among other things, specializes in designing wine labels. Beginning with the Gristina label in 1988, Michael has designed many of our local labels over the years. Along the way he has become friends with many of the wine people. His motivation to actually create his own label and open the winery was driven by a desire to preserve his neighboring land from development and to make the best use of his historic farm. Grateful neighbors share his vision.

Charles and Barbara Smithen
and Sherwood House Vineyards

As the wine industry grows on the North Fork, we are seeing the appearance of small operations that produce less than 2000 cases a year. The people who own these vineyards or wineries are an eclectic group who come into their business from many directions and for many reasons. They are also producing some of the best wines in our region.

Dr. Charles Smithen and his wife Barbara are a successful couple who absorbed the wine culture of southern France while staying

Barbara Smithen

at their vacation home in Antibes. It was a natural for them to buy a 38-acre farm on Oregon Road in Mattituck in which to retire. They are now living on their farm on the North Fork with 27 acres of grapes planted. Steve Mudd is their consulting vineyard manager and French winemaker Gilles Martin is their consulting winemaker. The wines are made at the Premium Group custom crush facility in Mattituck.

The Smithens, under the Sherwood House label, have produced some very high-quality wine. Their barrel-fermented Chardonnay is very Burgundian in character with rich fruit and a complex structure. Their reds have an elegant Bordeaux style and as a casual wine they make a "white Merlot" that is dry and just slightly pink in color. Barbara enjoys selling their wines on weekends out of their tiny tasting room on Elijah's Lane. She likes the personal relationship with her customers and the earthy feeling of working in the middle of the vineyard. Dr. Smithen is more interested in the science of wine and the artistry of making it. When personal pride plays such an important role in wine, the product can be pretty special. I think Sherwood House reflects that kind of pride.

Sherwood House tasting room

Jim and Linda Waters

The path to becoming a winemaker on the North Fork is long and arduous, with few tangible rewards except a bottle of fermented grape juice with your name on it. Normal people find it difficult to understand why someone would quit a lucrative job to own a small winery that spills out of a rented space in an industrial park. The word "passion" best describes the complex bundle of intangibles that is represented by that bottle and its label. Waters Crest is just such a winery.

Jim Waters grew up in Oyster Bay, where he graduated from high school in 1982. He went on to Nassau Community College where he played football for a championship team and graduated with a degree in hotel/restaurant management. He entered an internship program with Marriott hotels, working as a management trainee at the Uniondale Marriott and the Essex House in

Manhattan. During this time he learned about wine and its place in the hotel business. He had also spent a summer in France when in high school, experiencing first hand the culture of wine and food in the everyday lives of the French. As a successful athlete, Jim also tried out for a position on the New York Jets football team. He was cut from the team, but met someone who helped

Jim and Linda Waters

him get a job in the car rental business. This developed into a long and success-ful career with Avis, Budget Rent-a-Car, and as fleet manager for an oil company.

In 1988 Jim married Linda Minelli who, after graduation from college, became an air traffic controller. Coincidentally, she worked in the same office as North Fork wine pioneer Ray Blum. It was Linda who introduced Jim to Ray. It was also Linda's mother Lena who bought a home winemaking kit for Jim. Soon, one thing led to another, and Jim was making wine in his garage in Manorville and visiting Ray Blum in Cutchogue to help in the vineyard. He was further encouraged by a *Newsday* article written by Alan Wax about the gold medal he had won in a national home winemaking contest.

The garage operation in Manorville continued to grow. But Jim had a lot more going on than just working and making wine in his garage. He was a member of the Manorville volunteer fire department and was the elected commissioner for two terms. His family had long roots in the fire department in Oyster Bay. Jim and Linda were also raising a family that included two little girls.

The event that made Jim Waters leave his corporate career and open a small winery was the tragedy of the terrorist attack on the World Trade Center on September 11, 2001. He was sum-moned into the ruins after the attack along with many other volunteer firemen on Long Island. They were there to help out wherever needed and the enormity of the tragedy had a profound effect on Jim. Suddenly, traveling around the country and being away from his children didn't satisfy him, and the notion of opening his own winery had been floating in his head for a long time. In 2001 Waters Crest Winery was born.

Jim was passionate about making his own wine instead of having it made at a custom crush facility, so he leased space at the Cutchogue Commons industrial center and set up tanks and barrels to process his wine. He drew on his friends and contacts that he had made over the past ten years to buy premium grapes from Steve Mudd, Dick Pfeifle, Richie Pisacano and others. The unusual location was chosen because Jim foresaw selling his wine wholesale to restaurants and retail stores, but after a while he set up a small tasting room in the front of the winery and it began to grow.

Waters Crest wines started winning awards and developing a following. The addition of a barrel club where people would actually purchase a barrel and receive part of its contents over a four year period proved successful, as did a more traditional wine club. The intimate tasting room and winemaking facility made up in personal involvement with the winemaking and the personality of Jim Waters what it lost in ambiance. They are now producing over a thousand cases per year of a wide range of wines from their premium red blend called "Compania Rosso" to their Private Reserve Chardonnay to their Cabernet Franc.

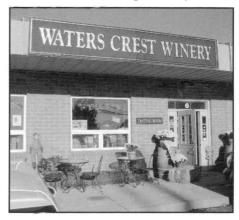

Jim and Linda Waters have now operated Waters Crest for seven years. They have experienced the joy of a newly released wine and agony of trying to pay the bills in a very expensive business. But the passion and the pride remain intact, as can be seen as soon as you start talking to them about those wines.

THE CHEF AS WINEMAKER;
FOOD ASSUMES AN EVER-GROWING ROLE

David Page and Barbara Shinn

The story of the life of David and Barbara, owners of Shinn Estate Vineyards, is the story of the American revolution in food and wine. From the birth of "California cuisine" to the wine explosion of Napa Valley, to the emergence of regional cuisine, to the production of fine wine from a bio-dynamic vineyard on the North Fork, they have experienced and been part of it all. They now feel that they represent the new generation of wineries in our region.

David is from Berlin, Wisconsin and Barbara is from Toledo, Ohio. He attended the University of Wisconsin for three years and hitchhiked to a new life in San Francisco. Arriving in 1979 when "nouvelle cuisine" was among the first signs of change in

Shinn Estate Vineyards

David Page

our food revolution, David took a job as a prep cook at a place called "Chez Moi." He was to work in many restaurants during the next ten years before becoming the head chef at a restaurant called FOTO. Barbara went to Miami University, where she graduated with a degree in fine arts. She then went on to the California College of the Arts in San Francisco where she earned a masters degree in fine arts. She was into the East Bay art scene and was specializing in abstract photography. She met David while he was cooking and she was dining at a restaurant in San Francisco.

The newly engaged couple made a decision to go to New York City and find a new life. But they took a slow, meaningful trip across country to get there. On the way they traveled the back roads and experienced up close the eating and living habits of the local people. I also think they discovered their own roots in the new context of their experience. At any rate, this trip had a big impact on their future endeavors. They wound up in New York full of energy and ideas, but broke. David got a cooking job at a place called the Box Tree and Barbara worked as a waitress. It was 1990 and they lived in a small apartment on Canal Street.

By 1993 they had saved a little money and were tired of working for others so they

Barbara Shinn

bought a small restaurant in Greenwich Village and called it "Home." At Home, they had a casual, neighborhood ambiance but cooked everything from scratch and bought from local purveyors. It was an immediate success. In fact, after being open only two weeks they were reviewed by Gael Greene and got rave reviews. Before long they started coming out to the North Fork and staying at a motel some days off, discovering the farmstands and wineries along the way. By 1996 they had the choice of buying an apartment in the city or purchasing a beautiful home on the Sound in Southold. They chose the latter and have now settled here permanently.

Their interest in selling local wine was inspired by Bob and Joyce Pellegrini when they brought a bottle of their wine to the Home restaurant. After that, they began exploring the wineries and had a private label custom wine made for their restaurant by Rich Olsen-Harbich. More custom wines were to follow. They purchased their 23-acre farm on Oregon Road in 1998 and began planting vines while still working at the restaurant in the city. The first wine they made from their own grapes was 450 cases from the 2002 vintage. Their "Young Vines" label got very high critical acclaim at a tasting on the East End, beating out many other established wineries in a blind tasting. And by 2006 they were able to produce their first vintage at their own winery in the newly renovated barns. They turned a small shed into a tasting room and completely renovated and expanded the farmhouse to make it into an Inn. They also planted more vines, now having the property filled with over 20 acres planted.

Aside from having a vineyard and winery that includes a small inn (the first of its kind on Long Island), they have set themselves apart by moving towards having a completely organic vineyard. Barbara especially has focused on moving from conventional, to sustainable, to organic, and finally to a bio-dynamic vineyard. She describes the land surrounding their vines as a pasture that hasn't been plowed up in 8 years. The natural growth under the vines plus the clover which she has planted create a green "manure" when mowed that leaves beneficial microbes to feed the soil. This is augmented with organic fertilizers derived from fish bones, seaweed, and a bio-dynamic compost called "compost tea." These are diluted with water and distributed through the drip irrigation system. Insects are minimized by the use of pheromone ties, bat houses, and a bacterium called B.T. The vineyard certainly has the look of a meadow with all the grasses and clover.

With production around 5000 cases per year, Shinn Estate Vineyard is really not all that small for our region. Anthony Nappa is their full-time winemaker, Barbara is the vineyard manager, and David oversees the whole operation. His background as a chef and restaurant owner make him uniquely qualified to understand the people who come to the tasting room and the inn, and his well developed palate enables him to detect the subleties in the wine. Most importantly, the passion that both Barbara and David have for the wine and the food is evident everywhere you look.

Christopher Tracy

There are advantages and disadvantages to working in a small, new, and relatively unknown wine region. People don't know much about our region and some who do feel that it lacks credibility. Our production is very small and our prices are perceived as a little high. But, lacking tradition and long-standing rules, we are free to experiment with different grape varieties, styles, and exotic blends. The past 35 years have shown that our climate and soil can produce excellent wine when handled properly. Channing Daughters Winery in Bridgehampton is an example of just how innovative a local winery can be. Christopher Tracy has an unusual background for a winemaker by traditional measures, but his enthusiasm and willingness to innovate have earned him high praise.

Christopher, a graduate of the French Culinary Institute in Manhattan, feels that a chef and winemaker have much in common. Both jobs, though highly romanticized in recent years, involve hard, often repetitive work. The cycle for a winemaker is spread over a year, or vintage, while the chef's cycle is much more compressed, ideally repeating itself daily. The chef uses a spice rack and fresh herbs to flavor the food, while the winemaker uses oak barrels and yeasts to create enticing flavors and aromas. Both the winemaker and the chef need an experienced palate and a respect for quality ingredients to succeed. And they both need a passion for their job.

Channing Daughters is really succeeding because of its team of artistic, dedicated people. The owner, Walter Channing, a renowned sculptor and business executive, knows when to leave people alone. Their CEO, Larry Perrine, is a Long Island wine pioneer and a highly respected winemaker and viticulturalist. He also has a very creative background and much formal education in viticulture. His vineyard manager, Abel Lopez, has been trained by Larry from the beginning. And Christopher, their young winemaker, brings the palate of a chef and the creative enthusiasm of an actor to the table. Allison,

Christopher and Allison Tracy

Christopher's wife, is the general manager who pays the bills and directs operations on a day-to-day basis. Larry, Christopher and Allison are all partners in the business with Walter Channing. Together, they produce about 12,000 cases of wine annually.

The winery in Bridgehampton is surrounded by 28 acres of grapes that include 12 different varieties. They purchase grapes from growers such as Steve Mudd and Sam McCullough on the North Fork from about an equal amount of acreage. Their labels are unusual and so are the wines — Sylvanus, Tocai Friulano, Cuvee Tropical, L'Enfant Sauvage, and Rosso Fresco to name a few. They create "field blends" that are designed to be blended while still in the vineyard. They make many wines in small batches of two or three hundred cases that almost seem like specials in a restaurant. They can do this because they have developed a cult-like wine club that is loyal and devoted. Christopher attaches great importance to the pairing of wines and food to the extent that he includes suggestions with the wines that are sent to wine club members. "Tocai is the quintessential prosciutto wine" is an example. A wine called "Over and Over"is red wine that has been "repassed" over a fresh vintage, aged, and repassed again. This rich blend, including Dornfelder, is said to be good with "grains, mushrooms, root vegetables, and game birds." This kind of innovation takes a creative mind and a clientele willing to experiment. Christopher seems to break every classic rule, but the wines are fresh and delicious.

THE VINEYARD MANAGER – AN UNSEEN HERO

The farmer evolves into a highly skilled professional, nurturing the vines in a difficult climate

If the winemaker is perceived as the chemist, then the vineyard manager is perceived as the farmer. It is a well known cliche that great wines begin in the vineyard. And most of the Long Island wineries produce estate-grown wines — wines that are produced with the wineries' own grapes. These grapes are tended by the "vigneron" or vineyard manager.

The vineyard manager is often never seen by the public and his (or her) picture is rarely in the press or on the bottle, but their ability to deliver good fruit year after year is critical. The choice of grape variety for a specific microclimate, the spacing of the vines, the trellis system used, the pruning and hedging decisions, and the methods of controlling mildew and pests — these are some of the issues facing the vineyard manager. More importantly, the relationship between the vineyard manager and the winemaker is critical. Ideally, the decision of when to harvest is a joint decision representing the desire of the winemaker for perfect fruit and the desire of the vineyard manager to get the fruit in before it is too late. The vineyard manager must work very hard twelve months a year to get to the point of harvest and takes great pride to produce good fruit vintage after vintage. And if the wine turns out to be delicious, we usually give the credit to the winemaker. Sometimes life is just not very fair.

Charlie Hargrave and Betty Cibulski

Charlie Hargrave is the quiet, serious, hard working vineyard mana-ger at Peconic Bay Vineyards. He was driving the tractor in 1973 when his older brother Alex and sister-in-law Louisa were riding on the back, planting the first vinifera wine grapes on Long

Island. Betty Cibulski joined the Hargraves a few years later, in 1984, and is now Charlie's assistant vineyard manager at Peconic Bay. Both of these people have a deep love of farming and viticulture. The process of nurturing each vine and its clusters of grapes through the season, no matter what Mother Nature has in store, motivates them as they try to produce the best fruit possible.

The Hargrave brothers grew up in Rochester, New York. While Alex went off to Princeton and later Harvard to study Asian culture and language, Charlie attended the Rochester Institute of Technology and was interested in woodworking, developing his skills with an eye to going into the furniture business. But while

Charlie Hargrave

still a student he came to Long Island to help out planting those first grapevines. There was much to learn in those early years as they got to know the soil and the microclimate of Cutchogue. The vines grew, and so did Charlie's knowledge of how to handle them. He ended up doing many different jobs at the early Hargrave Vineyard, including lots of repair work and carpentry. But he also developed a love of viticulture that has endured to this day.

After almost fifteen years in the vineyards of Hargrave, Charlie felt it was time for a change, so he left his job and moved to Virginia. His sister Meg lived there and her husband had a construction business. Charlie went to work for him and stayed there until the year 2000. Feeling the heat of the Virginia summer and missing the vineyards of the North Fork, he returned to Long Island, this time to become the vineyard manager at Peconic Bay Vineyards. It was an easy transition. The Hargrave Winery had been sold to the Borgheses and some of the old, familiar Hargrave employees were working at Peconic Bay. Greg Gove was the winemaker and Matt Gillies (who worked at Hargrave as a teenager) was the general manager. Soon after Charlie joined the team he was joined by longtime Hargrave employee, Betty Cibulski. At times it seems like a reincarnation of the Hargrave years, but it makes us realize how a relatively small body of skilled employees becomes the engine that drives our industry.

Betty Cibulski walked into the tasting room at Hargrave in 1984 with her son Todd. He was a young teen and she was trying to help find him a job. They were greeted by

Betty Cibulski

a lively and cheerful Louisa Hargrave who promptly inquired whether Betty herself would like to work there. Louisa asked her if she was "fast" and Betty said, "I don't know how to answer that." Her son agreed that she was fast and a hard worker. Louisa said that she would be "opening windows" and you had to be fast and thorough. What she meant by opening windows was leaf pulling, a necessary process to expose the grape clusters to air circulation and sunshine, thus reducing the powdery mildew and downey mold that harms the grapes. Betty eventually left her job as a nurse's aid and worked full time in the vineyards for the next 25 years.

Betty is not a native Long Islander, but a Canadian who was born in Halifax, Nova Scotia. She came from a farm family and was used to very hard work at an early age. Her American husband Jerry met her at a Canadian Tire store in Nova Scotia. They were married in 1965 and moved to Massachusetts, where her husband worked for Agway. After he was transferred to Long Island they settled down on the North Fork. Charlie and Betty supervise a crew of four full-time workers and take care of 55 acres of vines which are located around the winery on Main Road and on Oregon Road to the North. After all of these years of hard labor, Betty still finds pleasure in looking at the vine and figuring out the canes for the next vintage.

Richie Pisacano

The Hargraves were about to release the first vinifera wine on Long Island. It was 1976. The New York Times, The New Yorker, and Newsday were all excitedly anticipating this event. But out of the stage lights was Dave Mudd and his son Steve who had also been growing vinifera since 1974. They went on to become a virtual training center for future vineyard managers. One of their early graduates was Richie Pisacano. He is now the owner of the artisanal Roanoke Vineyards and the vineyard manager for Wolffer Estate Vineyards.

Richie is a local boy who graduated from Southold High School in 1980. Even before that, in 1977, he was apprenticing with the Mudds. In high school, Richie developed an interest in horticul-

Richie and Soraya Pisacano

ture and especially in plant propagation. The idea of making new plants out of old ones seemed like a fascinating subject. He furthered his studies at Suffolk Community College and continued working for Dave and Steve Mudd. In the late 1970's lots of people came to ask their advice about planting a vineyard. This was how the Mudd's consulting business was born. Richie remembers planting the first vineyard for Dr. Damianos at Pindar; he also planted Cutchogue Vineyard which later became Gristina; and he remembers planting the first vines at Palmer. These were exciting times and Richie was able to learn as the region grew.

In 1982 Richie left his job with the Mudds and started his own nursery business that specialized in grafting grape vines. This is a technique where existing grape stocks are used to change the variety of grapes on a vine. Richie was one of the grafting pioneers in our area. He was only 22 years old. But soon he encountered a slowing down of business and the pressure of having to market his product. He left his grafting business and bought a piece of property on Herricks Lane in Jamesport. On this 15-acre piece of land he eventually planted 12 acres of Chardonnay and Merlot grapes. Over the next 17 years he worked this vineyard and sold the grapes to the wineries. In 2000 Richie sold his Jamesport vineyard and settled into building his own tasting room and 7-acre vineyard in Riverhead. This was the birth of Roanoke Vineyards. Richie also took the full time job of vineyard manager at Wolffer Estate Vineyards in Bridgehampton.

I asked Richie if, after all these years tending the vines, he feels that our area has the qualities to make great wine. He said "absolutely!" He said that we can only compete on the quality market. He also said that in this marginal, cool climate environment we have to have precise vineyard management where we are careful about yields and accurate with our goals. The early pioneers didn't always put the vineyard as their number one priority. The wineries and all the equipment that went in them often consumed the budget and stole the limelight. But intensive care is required to make world class wine. Richie said "what you reap is what you sell".

What does that "intensive care" actually mean today? It means the use of VSP (vertical shoot positioning) where the fruit is on the low wire of a vertical trellis. The wires have to be constantly raised to accommodate the growing vines, and the leaves have to be hedged to allow the proper amount of sun exposure. It's a very labor-intensive system that, if done properly, allows the grapes of one variety to develop uniformly so that they ripen at the same time. Also, you cannot be afraid to "drop" grapes when necessary. That's how great wine is made.

What about the ideal soil for grape growing? Well, it depends upon the grape variety, according to Richie. We started to believe that vines like light, weak soil. This results in highly stressed vines with low vigor and early ripening. It also means good drainage. But Richie Pisacano feels that Merlot likes a friendlier soil with more nutrients and water-holding capacity. It should be irrigated because it doesn't like to go through spikes of stress. When Merlot is grown in a comfortable environment, it produces wines with depth and longevity.

After years of growing grapes for others, Richie Pisacano takes great pride in having his own wines under the Roanoke label. His wines are actually made by Roman Roth, his longtime colleague at Wolffer. The red grapes are grown on his own vineyard in Riverhead, which he feels is especially suited for the long ripening required of Cabernet Sauvignon. He buys his Chardonnay grapes from Dave Mudd's vineyard in Southold, where his career began. Richie feels that he has learned by watching some of the mistakes of others.

A model started to unfold that was about being small and artisanal. Making enough to sustain the farm with hard work and eliminating all the things that make it difficult. No great illusion, just small quantities of great wine. He and his wife Soraya only sell their wine from their tasting room. They limit their wine club to 100 members so that they can keep it personal — and fun.

Dave Thompson

Dave Thompson was born in Hartford, Connecticut and graduated from Syracuse University. He then worked in commercial horticulture. But in 1980 he was doing some carpentry work for Richard Ressler in Boston when Richard and his brother purchased land on Eastern Long Island. In 1981 he came to Cutchogue, and helped plant 22 acres of grapes at a time when the wine industry was just getting started. Neither he nor the Resslers had any experience with vineyards, but according to Dave, they "talked to a lot of people." Ressler Vineyards went on to become one of the prime sources for premium grapes on the North Fork. Eventually it grew to 40 acres and was sold to Palmer Winery.

Dave Thompson

In 1985 Dave Thompson became the vineyard manager for Kip Bedell at his newly formed Bedell Cellars Winery. Now, 23 years later, Dave is still there. He says that the rewards of his job are long-term. Finding a way of farming on Long Island that works has been a great satisfaction and helps to create something that will "outlive myself." A quiet, laid back personality, Dave doesn't mind working under the radar. "When it works, it's because of a team effort, when everyone has their part to play."

Dave's part has been an important one. He plans the progression of events that lead to a successful harvest each year. Each step affects the others and every change causes long term effects. Dave says "unlike California, we really have vintages here." During the dead of winter the vines are dormant. That's when the pruning is done. From bud break in May until veraison (color change) in August, things are very busy in the vineyard. Buds are removed from the trunks (suckering) and the shoots tied to the trellis wires. The vines are trained to grow upright in a system called VSP (vertical shoot positioning). As the leaves (or canopy) proliferates, they have to be trimmed along the sides and top. This is done with a mechanical hedger and it creates the optimum amount of sun exposure for the grapes and reduces the negative effects of too much moisture. The goal is to develop a desirable crop load for each vineyard section and each grape variety. Dave says that much of it is "serendipity" — you don't know what a particular site is going to give you until it is in the barrel. At Bedell Cellars they are fortunate to have enough tank capacity to keep each block of grapes separate through fermentation and aging. The various components are eventually blended to create a balanced wine.

When asked if he believes that, after 30 years of growing vinifera grapes, our region is really special, Dave says yes. The sandy, well drained soil and unique maritime climate produce flavors unlike any others. Long Island wines have a distinctive character all their own. And he is very proud to be part of this heritage.

Sam McCullough

Sam McCullough is an educated, sophisticated farmer who knows grapevines. In 1989 he joined winemaker Eric Fry as his vineyard manager and they have been together ever since. He will show you the thick and gnarled root stock that was planted in the 1970's. Above that is the graft union where the Gewurztraminer varietal was joined to the phylloxera-resistant native root. Above the graft union is the scion which includes the head, the canes, the tendrils, the leaves, and the perfectly ripened grape clusters. It requires skill, good judgement, and much work to bring this vine to fruition. Sam manages 50 acres of Lenz grapes plus another 16 of his own.

Sam is the son of Dr. Norman McCullough and his wife Linda. He has lived on the North Fork his whole life, graduating from Mattituck High School in 1978. He knew he wanted to be a farmer since working for Bruno Orlowski as a student. Sam went off to college at Colorado State University in Fort Collins, Colorado. He majored in horticultural food production and studied chemistry, agronomy, and soil science. He graduated in 1983 and returned to the North Fork to work for Dave Mudd. 1983 was a very active time in the vineyards of the North Fork. The industry was very young and growing rapidly. Dave Mudd's vineyard management company was busy planting over 100 acres of new vines in that year alone. It was a good time for Sam to learn about vines.

After leaving Mudd's consulting operation in 1986, Sam worked for Pindar for 6 months before opening a vineyard management business of his own. He managed vineyards for various clients, including Southold Vineyard, which went on to become Corey Creek. Peter Carroll became a client with Lenz vineyards before Sam became a full-time employee in 1989. After an initial period when Sam and Eric didn't always see eye to eye, they became a formidable team based on knowledge and trust. It has often been said that Eric works with some of the best fruit on the island. That is because of the care and hard work that Sam puts into it.

In 1991, Sam and his father, Dr. McCullough, bought 20 acres of land on Tuthills Lane in Aquebogue. Gradually, year by year, they planted 16 acres of grapes, predominantly Merlot, on this property. Sam believes that the Merlot grape is the most perfectly suited to our climate on the North Fork, although many other varieties do very well. He feels that the topography of a particular vineyard is very important because vines like high, well drained soil with good water and air circulation. The long, temperate fall is ideal to let the grape ripen slowly, developing soft tannins and complex flavors. He constantly

Sam McCullough

examines the grape clusters, dropping grapes when necessary to achieve an average 2½-ton-per-acre harvest for Merlot. But it is Eric, the winemaker, who makes the final decision on when to harvest the grapes. Harvest time is always intense and very stressful because the weather is so unpredictable. And having grapes that have been beautifully cared for is a winemakers dream.

Peter Gristina

Peter Gristina is the son of Dr. Jerry Gristina of Larchmont, NY. In 1984 Dr. Gristina and Bob Pelligrini purchased 54 acres of land in Cutchogue and had grapes planted on it. In 1987 the partners had a falling out and Dr. Gristina became the sole proprietor of

Kathy and Peter Gristina

the new Gristina Winery. The vineyard was planted by Steve Mudd. Peter worked with Steve in the vineyard during his summer vacations from college. He graduated from George Washington University in 1985 and came to work full time at the winery. Larry Perrine started as a consultant and became the full time winemaker in 1988. Peter went on to become the vineyard manager and worked closely with Larry. The first vintage of Gristina wine was released in 1988.

But this beautiful property on the main road just west of Cutchogue village has a long history of turmoil. After Jerry Gristina split with his business partner Bob Pelligrini, he eventually split with his wife Carol. Just two months before Peter was to get married in 1992, he found out about the divorce. The winery and vineyard went into receivership and Peter was appointed as general manager. It was a difficult time for him and he was placed under a lot of stress: he was working seven days a week; his first child was born in 1994; and Larry Perrine quit in 1994. Peter had to train a new manager, John Perry, and his father's new wife, Marygail. Finally, Peter left in 1997, choosing to spend more time with his growing family. Charles Flatt was hired as winemaker, followed by Adam Suprenant. By 2001 Gristina Vineyards was sold to Vince Gallucio, who re-christened it Gallucio Family Wineries. Peter didn't know about the sale until he read it in the papers. Vince Gallucio sold the property to the Macari family in 2007.

Peter says that "for me it's ancient history and I don't dwell on it. We planted a great vineyard at Gristina and I learned a lot over my 16 years." In the fall of 1999 Peter went to work for Dr. Damianos as the vineyard manager at Duck Walk Vineyards in Water Mill. He has now worked at Duck Walk for nine years, managing 130 acres of grapes. The acreage is spread out between five locations, four on the North Fork and one in Water Mill. He takes pride in producing a clean, viable crop year after year no matter what the weather throws at him. Duck Walk produces about 30,000 cases per year of mostly estate-bottled wine.

Ben Sisson

When Ben Sisson was still a student at Riverhead High School, he worked part-time at the Cornell research farm nearby. This was the late 1970's and vineyard research was in its early stages on the North Fork. Ben was introduced to what would become his lifelong career — vineyard management. He was an example of a local person who developed hands-on skills in our wine industry and emerged as a respected professional in the vineyard. Along the way he married Alice Wise, viticulture specialist for Cornell Cooperative Extension, and worked with many people in the wine community.

Ben Sisson

Ben's first full-time job in viticulture was at Pindar in 1982. They were just beginning in what would become Long Island's largest winery. Ben worked with Bruce Pinneo and Mark Chen in the production of Long Island Winter White, a wine that became famous as an introduction to wine for many people around the Island. It was made from the hybrid grape Cayuga and was inexpensive, deliciously fruity, and slightly sweet. It is still being sold today after more than 25 years of production.

Ressler Vineyards, just west of Pugliese, provided the first vineyard manager job for Ben in 1984. Kirk and Richard Ressler owned the vineyard of about 40 acres, which is not well known outside the industry because they never built their own winery, but among insiders was a highly respected source for buying grapes. They grew Chardonnay, Riesling, Merlot, and Cabernet Sauvignon, selling them to Long Island wineries such as Bridgehampton and to other wineries such as Crosswoods Vineyards in Connecticut. In 1996 Ressler vineyard was sold to Palmer. It was partially due to the fact that it is difficult to make a profit just selling grapes. They are expensive to produce, and the contracts to sell them are often difficult to enforce because of the unpredictability of each vintage.

Ben went on to work for Dave and Steve Mudd, whose vineyard management company has planted and maintained more grapevines than anyone else. Ben feels that the Mudds had a far more wide-ranging influence on Long Island wine than the Hargraves, and without them our region would never have become what it is today. While working for the Mudds, Ben helped to plant the vineyards for Raphael, Ackerman, Dr. Smithen, and Russell McCall, among others. He left Mudd Vineyards in 2000 to become vineyard manager for Raphael, working with Richard Olsen-Harbich. During this time, Ben developed his own palate and learned how specific decisions in the vineyard translate into tastes in the bottle. He also met Paul Pontalier, from Chateau Margaux, who came to the winery three or four times a year as a consultant.

After Raphael, Ben Sisson was hired as vineyard manager for Russell McCall, who owns a twenty-acre vineyard on Main Road in Cutchogue and has been growing Pinot Noir and Merlot for about 10 years. Russell is in the process of producing his own ultra-premium wines and will be releasing them soon.

With his years of experience, Ben joined the ranks of fellow vineyard managers who have learned the intricacies of growing grapes on the North Fork — and have learned of the idiosyncrasies of their owners. *Author's note: sadly, Ben Sisson died on January 24, 2009 after a sudden illness. He was 49 years old.*

THE TASTING ROOM TAKES ON INCREASED SIGNIFICANCE

The Tasting Room Manager

Many people have worked in winery tasting rooms since 1976. They are a diverse group of interesting employees who come from many educational, experiential and cultural backgrounds. Much like a bartender in a busy tavern, they have to be friendly, entertaining and responsible. They also have to have a good knowledge of wine and how it is made.

In the 1980's many of the tasting rooms on Long Island consisted of a small counter in an old potato barn. One employee would give visitors tasting portions of their wines, usually for free. But Pindar Vineyards began giving organized tours on a daily basis. Dr. Damianos was the original tour guide, and he trained many others to follow.

The tours became very popular and well-attended. At the end of the tour the visitors would end up in the tasting room, often very anxious to taste (and buy) the wines described on the tour. Other wineries developed tours, some led by the winemaker, who would lead the people through the complex process of winemaking, tasting samples at each stage of production. And some took people out into the vineyard to discover how the vines were nurtured as they approached harvest time.

Gradually, small gifts were added to the tasting room so that people could take home a souvenir other than wine. Corkscrews, embossed glasses, books, and logo T-shirts became popular. As the holidays approached, custom gift baskets containing wine, cheese, biscuits, and jellies were added to the inventory. Tasting room staff would assemble them and ship them all over the country.

Tasting rooms became more sophisticated with the addition of art shows, book signings, musical events, and cooking demonstrations. With groups of people arriving in limousines and buses, the demand for entertainment grew, and outdoor picnic facilities and live music were added.

Finally, the most recent growth has taken place in the development of the wine club. With the aid of technology in e-mail communication and computerized billing, wineries are able to enroll many new followers and give them incentives to buy. This has opened up a new area of marketing called subscription sales. Some wineries now need a wine club manager, an event manager, and a gift shop manager, in addition to the traditional tasting room manager.

The once-sleepy tasting room with a single attendant has become a thriving center of activity during the weekends throughout most of the year. The job of managing all this activity has become much more sophisticated and demanding, but the ultimate goal of selling the wine hasn't changed.

Jane Utz

When Jane Utz learned that Alex and Louisa Hargrave were about to make wine in Cutchogue, she was immediately captured by the excitement and romance of it all. Jane was a respected physical education teacher in Southold and Greenport from 1967 until she retired from the classroom in 1992. But since 1975 she has spent her summers and weekends in the tasting room, witnessing the first generation of Long Island wine from a vantage point that few others can claim.

Working at Hargrave Winery from 1975 until 1978 was an adventure that repeated itself every day. Each task in the vineyard, the winery, or the tasting room was pretty much uncharted territory. At that time, Alex and Louisa depended upon many part-timers who wanted to share the excitement of this new venture but had little expertise. Jane went home at night and pored over books to learn the mysteries of wine.

But it was not until 1985 that Jane Utz really found her niche in the growing Long Island wine industry. She accepted a job at Pindar and joined Dr. Damianos in becoming a tour guide. The charisma of the Doctor and the enthusiastic teaching ability of Jane created a phenomenon that has yet to be equalled. Groups were led through the vineyard, the crush pad, the fermenting tanks, and the barrel aging cellars. Finally they emerged into the tasting room full of excitement and the desire to taste all of these special wines. Of course they left with bottles (and cases) under their arms. It was market- ing through education at its best. Jane Utz contin- ued to lead tours and work in the tasting room at Pindar for the next 10 years, perfecting the art of the tour and the role of the tast- ing room associate.

Jane Utz

In 1995, Jane left Pindar and worked in the tasting rooms of Jamesport, Raphael, and Macari before settling in at Pugliese Wincry, located on the Main Road in Cutchogue. Jane brought profession- alism to the tasting room, and helped them prepare for the changing nature of the business.

Tongue in Cheek — by Jane Utz (*The GrapeZine*, 1994)

I've watched the experts deal with wine, the subject's quite confusing.

The things they say, the things they do, I still find most amusing.

I'm sure it's grapes they grow for wine, but the experts taste, then swear

That in that glass that came from vines are cherries, apple, pear...

And watch out for those fancy names (you may need a French primer)

Just order with authority: I'll have the gurtz-en-heimer!

But restaurants pose a greater threat with the list placed by your fork.

They offer some ancient ritual and make you smell the cork!

You must talk about the "nose" of wine, then swirl, that's real wine class.

I think the "nose" is to my left 'cause his is in the glass.
Wines are silky, soft, or buttery. They're chewy, chocolate, mint.
They're smoky, soapy, stemmy; Is this something I can drink?
Wine is flabby, musty, corky, unobtrusive, curt, and sassy;
It's approachable, closed-in, and tight; It's too young, and tough and nasty.
It's delicate and intricate, complex, simple, balanced; Introvert and pushy;
It needs a psychoanalyst! No matter what the experts say I refuse to be a phony
So when I want a pleasant white I order up the char-donney.
And if Robert Parker says it's good, or even if it's not
When I want a glass of big red wine I'll order the Merlot;
And for a pasta wine, I've found it's always my best bet
To order something heavy-perhaps the Cabernet.
All these wines I've found taste good; I understand...and yet
The experts say these wines are dry
But I'd swear the stuff's still wet!

Betsy Weiss

Among the small group of veterans who managed the tasting rooms on the North Fork for 15 years or more, no one was more active than Pindar tasting room manager Betsy Weiss. During her tenure from 1988 until 2003, no tasting room had as much traffic as Pindar. Hiring and training employees, replenishing the wine, keeping unruly customers in check, and guarding the cash register was Betsy's job. She also became involved in handling sales through the four distributors that sold Pindar wine in surrounding states.

Betsy is a 1981 graduate of Garden City High School. She went to the two-year Green Mountain College in Vermont before transferring to Adelphi University, where she graduated in 1985 as a business major. She had visited cousins on the North Fork as a kid and her father bought a piece of property on Nassau Point in 1988. It was that summer that Betsy came out and was hired by Barbara Hofer to be a tour guide at Pindar. She has been here ever since.

Dr. Damianos believes that educating the public about wine is the best way to sell it. Betsy reflects that "in the old days the Doctor and Jane Utz (and others) would lead the tours and I would provide the fun." Going to Pindar became so much fun that people told their friends about it and started coming out, not for a quick visit, but to spend the day. The fact that, at the time, the wine tasting was free helped a little too.

Back about 1990 the Long Island Railroad developed a package tour on Sunday mornings in which people would take the train from the city to Ronkonkoma, get on a bus (a yellow school bus) and ride the bus to the green in Cutchogue, where they would be given a cup of coffee. From there they would all go to Pindar for a tour of the winery. This was before our industry learned how to prepare for groups; the first thing they needed upon arrival was a restroom. Pindar had a small one off the lobby, but when the buses arrived the line would back into the parking lot. They now have spacious restrooms located behind the winery.

Betsy Weiss

Dealing with the little practical problems of life can be a challenge to a tasting room manager. Those bus tours became much more sophisticated over time. The heightened focus on DWI helped support the limo business, as did the discovery that a day trip for the bride-to-be — otherwise known as the bachelorette party — was a fun idea. Betsy (and all other veterans) agree that the bachelorette party was the work of the Devil. The betrothed, accompanied by 8 or 10 friends, would go from winery to winery, tasting many wines as they went. By the end of the day, these nice, fun-loving women had lost all inhibitions, were often very drunk, and could disrupt an entire winery.

Betsy Weiss was also insrumental in organizing the harvest festival, one of the most successful events on the East End. It all began in 1990 with Betsy and Mike Ryan, Pindar's general manager at the time. They borrowed a tent, got some bales of hay, and hired an "oompah band" dressed in lederhosen to play on a flatbed wagon. Meanwhile, Betsy cooked sausage and peppers over a grill. This first harvest festival was not a big success, but before long the bands grew better, the food was catered, and the crowds began to come. Each year, people told their friends about it, and the weekend after Columbus Day became so busy that it was all the staff could handle.

Since then, many of the wineries have developed similar events. The Long Island Wine Council has sponsored such favorites as barrel tastings and Windows on Long Island, giving winery employees a chance to get to know each other. Even though it was a lot of work, everyone looked forward to them.

Betsy was no exception, and has fond memories of being part of this "family." By 2003, Betsy felt that she was getting a "little burnt out" by it all and has since taken a quieter job in a wine and liquor store. She still promotes our local wine and shares her stories with others.

Bachelorette Party

Sue Skrezek

Sue Skrezek was a single mom in 1987 when she applied for a job in the tasting room at Palmer. She had no wine experience and was just grateful that Bob Palmer hired her. That was the beginning of an 18-year career at Palmer. She is now working at Raphael Winery in Peconic and is one of the most experienced tasting room people on the North Fork.

According to Sue, working in a tasting room is hard work. Setting up, cleaning up, and carrying back-breaking cases of wine — and that's before any people enter the picture.

Sue Skrezek

Sue says that the harvest season is the most active and describes it as "eight weeks of hell." At Palmer, hundreds of people would come to the winery, many to spend the day. With a band on the deck and hayrides for the kids, it was the perfect place to have a picnic. Wine was only sold by the glass for immediate consumption and guests were not allowed to bring in their own beverages. As the popularity of buses and limousines increased, these rules became necessary. Sue was concious of the fact that a winery is a place selling alcohol, and proper safeguards must be in place.

At Palmer in the 1990's, they created a series of poetry readings called "Voices on the Vine" that brought such famous poets as Robert Bly, Robert Creeley, and David Axelrod to the North Fork. They also had book signings with authors such as Nelson DeMille and others. These cultural events didn't always result in large wine sales, but they added a new dimension to the wineries and introduced more people to the ambiance of a vineyard. Sue Skrezek feels grateful to have been a part of the growing wine industry. As the daughter of an old North Fork farm family, she also feels good to be a part of keeping the North Fork green.

Bill Thompson

The tasting rooms on the North Fork have attracted many people as employees, with diverse backgrounds and reasons for taking the job. Bill Thompson was a marketing executive with Sears Roebuck & Co. for 25 years before taking early retirement. He is a graduate of Davidson College and the Wharton School of Business. He also served as an officer in the U.S. Navy. He did not have roots on the North Fork, originally coming from Alabama. But through a friend, and due to some business trips to Long Island, he discovered the beautiful agricultural nature of the North Fork. Bill took a part-time job at Bedell Cellars in 1990 and spent the next 16 years working there. He loves the North Fork and never plans to leave.

In 1990 Bedell Cellars had only been selling wine for five years. Bill Thompson had little wine experience but lots of knowledge

as a retailer. He was trained in the tiny Bedell tasting room by Cynthia Fuller and Susan Johnson. They emphasized that it was all about the wine. If you learn as much as you can about the wine, the rest will take care of itself. Bill did that and became the tasting manager as time went on. He also became part of a team that included vineyard manager Dave

Bill Thompson

Thompson, and winemaker/owner Kip Bedell. They worked closely together for years, helping to make Bedell Cellars one of the best and most respected wineries on the North Fork.

In the early days at Bedell, the tasting room consisted of a small wooden bar in the front of a renovated potato barn. The tanks and barrels were visible right behind the tasting area and the staff often consisted of one person. The budget was so small that if they needed something they usually tried making it themselves. But the excitement flowing in the new wine industry and the pride everyone took in the new Bedell wines made up for what they lacked in money. The customers who came to the winery at that time were just as excited to learn all they could about these new wines.

During the 1990's the tasting room staff remained small and winery events were few and far between. Bedell staged an annual vertical tasting of all their Merlots, held an annual picnic, and participated in various Wine Council doings such as barrel tastings and Windows on Long Island. Gradually, more people would come to the winery in groups. If they had reservations they would be given tours and provided with other amenities.

With the advent of tourism, Bedell's little tasting room has evolved into an entertainment center that functions more like a tavern than a wine tasting room. Like many wineries, it now requires reservations and has security guards added to the staff to maintain discipline.

Bill Thompson has enjoyed helping to preach the message of Long Island wine. Bedell wines keep getting better, and many more events are planned for the winery, both private and those open to the public. Bill is an example of a long-time winery employee who has made a great contribution to our community.

Nickolas Abramo

Nickolas Abramo is a former "army brat" who grew up on or near military bases around the world. But his grandfather, Willard Listing, owned a home on the Sound in Peconic. Over the years Nick enjoyed visiting his grandfather and fell in love with the North Fork. When Nick was nine years old, they visited the newly opened Hargrave Vineyard, where they bought a bottle of Pinot Noir signed by Alex Hargrave himself.

Years later, after his grandfather died, Nick's family moved into the old house in Peconic. In the summer of 1992, when he was a student at Georgia Southern University, his parents were transferred to Germany and Nick came north to take care of the house. He took a job in the tasting room of Lenz, and remained there as a full-time employee until 2006. His primary job was tasting room manager, but he ended up doing everything from pruning the vines to organizing the computer system.

Initially Nickolas had no experience with wine but his theater background helped him relate to the customers and sell the wine.

Nickolas Abramo

Lenz was growing and had just assembled the team that was to remain in place for years — Eric Fry, winemaker; Sam McCullough, vineyard manager; and Tom Morgan, sales manager.

After some intense education from all three of the above and a wine course with Kevin Zraly, Nick. became the retail arm of this team. Perhaps the most important contribution of owner Peter Carroll to the production of quality wine was to assemble these professionals and let them pursue their passion. Lenz has remained small and intensely focused on its wines at a time when new marketing initiatives have sometimes ventured away from the business of making quality wine.

Nickolas Abramo was part of the mid-1990's growth when Lenz "Old Vines" wines surpassed famous old world labels in blind tastings in New York. He was also a part of the very successful Chardonnay Classic and Merlot Classic held at Lenz during this time.

In the late 1990's, other quality wineries were following Lenz in producing some very good wine and stepping up the competition. But Lenz stuck to its plan and conservative style. Nick began supplementing his income by working part-time at the Seafood Barge, growing into the job of beverage director. He was instrumental in developing one of the best local wine lists on the North Fork. Nick has been one of those behind-the-scenes people who have made the wine industry work.

Barbara Reuschle

Barbara Reuschle is the current tasting room manager at Lenz. She replaced Nickolas when he went on to a job as a country club manager in 2001. Barbara is a friendly, outgoing person who enjoys drinking wine and talking about it. Her wine education was enhanced by Lenz winemaker Eric Fry. When customers come into Lenz, Barbara wants the wine tasting experience to be both fun and educational. She asks them if they want to taste the Estate Flight or the Premium Flight. The Estate Flight is priced at $5 per person and includes five of Lenz's seven estate wines.

The pouring order starts with Gewurztraminer due to its distinctive taste and lingering aromas. It is followed by the Blanc de Noir which is light with lively acidity. It not only tastes refreshing to start, but cleans the palate for the wines to follow. Then comes the White Label Chardonnay, the Gold Label Chardonnay, the Merlot, Cabernet Sauvignon, and the Estate Merlot. The portions are about one ounce and the tastings are sometimes shared by two people. Tasting sheets are provided for notes and comparisons. The Premium Flight costs $10 and allows you to taste their "Old Vines" series. These wines, which include Chardonnay, Merlot, Cabernet Sauvignon, and an aged sparkling wine called RD, are the winery's best and since they are only

Barbara Reuschle

made in good vintage years, their availability is limited to wine club members.

Lenz, like many of its competitors, has an active wine club that customers are encouraged to join. The club consists of three levels, each one requiring a larger committment but offering greater rewards. Level 1 requires four shipments per year and the expenditure of about $400. In return, members receive a 15% discount on all purchases of the Estate wines. The Level 2 member is obligated to purchase one case of Old Vines wine per year and they receive a 25% discount on all purchases of Estate wines. The Level 3 member purchases one mixed case of Old Vines wine per quarter and receives a 33% discount.

Club members are offered many perks throughout the year such as special wine and food events, private tastings, and the use of a cottage for overnight visits. In general, wine clubs have been very popular throughout the industry because they result in increased sales for the winery and a way to reward regular customers for their patronage.

Lois Ross

Lois Ross is a part-time tasting room assistant who works the front line of the tasting room at Lenz. She enjoys the people who come

Lois Ross, with unidentified customer

there, seeking knowledge about wine and the fun of comparative tasting. Customers come from all over the New York area and beyond, with wide-ranging levels of wine experience and many unusual perceptions. Dealing with them requires lots of patience, tact, and the ability to keep it fun. It also helps to be familiar with the North Fork and its people.

Lois knows a great many people on the East End well, due to her restaurant and musical careers, and the customers love to come in and chat about everything local. When it comes to wine, some people are serious connoisseurs who might be comparing vintages from various wineries to find the "best" wine, while others have never tasted good wine at all, and are just looking for a relaxing time in the country. For the latter, Lenz provides picnic tables where one can sit down, purchase a bottle of wine, have some local goat cheese with crackers, and enjoy the afternoon.

Barbara Hofer

Barbara is a Long Islander who was born in Farmingdale and has now been on the North Fork for many years. She took a job in the tasting room of Pindar in 1985 with no special knowledge or even interest in wine. Like many others, she just needed a job. But at Pindar she learned about wine, first with winemaker John Jaffray and later with Bob Henn. She learned from Dr. Damianos how to conduct the tours and work the tasting room.

Now, in 2009, Barbara still enjoys the tasting room customers, trying to "read" each of them to determine their level of interest and expertise. Since 2002 she has been working for Macari Vineyards and has become an important part of their management team. The tasting room is very upscale with a beautiful ambiance and a large deck overlooking the vineyard. The inventory of wine starts from a $10 wine called "Collina" to a $100 bottle of limited production red called "Solo Uno".

Since 2003, Barbara has been in charge of developing a wine club that now has over 1000 people signed up. The members are

Barbara Hofer

required to receive four shipments a year that range in price from $50-$65 each. They receive a 20% discount on additional purchases and are able to enjoy free tastings at the winery plus many other perks and amenities. The winery has subscribed to a computerized billing system called "Wine Direct" that streamlines the whole purchasing process. The popularity of the wine club has increased sales and tasting room traffic immensely, with many of the wine club members introducing friends to the winery.

Barbara Hofer is definitely a person who enjoys interacting with people, and it shows in the way she handles customers at the winery. She is an example of the successful tasting room person who can communicate the passion of wine — even to the novice visitor who doesn't have a clue.

THE EVENT PLANNERS AND THE TOUR BUSINESS

Ben Coutts, Keri McKillop and Others

Ben Coutts and Keri McKillop are just two examples of wine people who have been instrumental in making wineries into more than a place to buy wine — they are event planners who encourage and organize people to use the beautiful settings and ambiance of the wineries as venues for all kinds of parties and celebrations. This segment of the business started slowly, and of course many people have been involved in marketing. The event planners play a vital role in the wineries' use of special events as a source of revenue.

Ben was hired by Bob Pellegrini as their general manager in 1998. His first assignment was "The Kitchen at Pellegrini," an ambitious series of chef cooking demonstrations and wine tasting. David Page began the series and was followed by others, including Eberhardt Mueller and myself. It was a big success and gave exposure to Long Island food and wine. It also started a debate over whether wineries should be allowed to have kitchen facilities and be able to serve food. Health department regulations, town ordinance and zoning rules came into play. The real problem is that it is impossible to separate wine from food and we just have

Ben and Karen Coutts

to adapt the rules to the reality. Ben Coutts then moved on to Martha Clara, where he worked under general manager Bob Kearn

Martha Clara was the first winery actually designed for events, from the spacious tasting room, to the nearby pavilion, to the demonstration kitchens and art gallery. They had even made provisions for adequate restrooms and parking. Ben and Bob Kearn would create events, and then take the responsibility of filling them and making sure they went smoothly. At times, the wine seemed secondary, but they did teach others how to bring people to the vineyard.

Over at Palmer they were well into their series of poetry readings called "Voices on the Vine," which were organized by winemaker Tom Drozd and local poet Dan Murray. Later, at Borghese Vineyards, they instituted live opera performances performed by the Hamptons Opera Company. Culturally, this was successful, but for events to work they have to be "about the wine," or close to it.

As time went on, the events multiplied and fell into three broad categories. First, the weddings, parties, and fund raisers. In this type of event, the winery merely rents out the premises for the evening. They are basically selling their ambiance and view — and hopefully a little wine. All catering, tents, chairs, tables, and amenities are brought in from outside. Some wineries hired event planners like Ben Coutts to coordinate all the purveyors involved.

The second category of events are in-house. The motive for these is not so much profit as it is exposure and education. Years ago, Kip Bedell began doing an annual vertical tasting of all his Merlots. A little bread and cheese were served. Bridgehampton introduced a Chardonnay Classic in which Chardonnays from all over the world were tasted along with our local ones. Peter Carroll followed this up with a Merlot Classic along the same lines. Many other in-house events have included wine and food pairing, chef's demonstrations and vineyard tours.

The third category of events would be those sponsored by the Long Island Wine Council or other groups. The barrel tastings in the 1990's were enormously popular. A big tent in the field at Hargrave Vineyard, Starr Boggs as the chef, with chargrilled swordfish, lobster, and corn-on-the-cob for 1000 people. After 5 or 6 of these, some of the glow wore off. The expenses increased, major sponsors (such as the *Wine Spectator*) backed out, and the health department stepped in. The other major industry-wide event was Windows on Long Island. Initially held at the World Trade Center in '90,'91, and '92, it was suspended when the trade center was bombed in 1993. It was moved to South Street Seaport, Gustavino's, and Capitale before coming to an end in 2000. These industry-wide events took an enormous amount of organization, much of it handled by Jane Baxter-Lynn, the director of the wine council before Steven Bate.

Keri McKillop graduated with a business degree from Hunter College and went on for a Masters Degree at New Paltz. She worked as an events coordinator for CBS television, where she was part of the Winter Olympics in Lillehammer, Norway, coordinating trips for sponsors. When she wanted to be closer to her family she moved to the East End and went to work for Pellegrini Vineyards.

Keri McKillop

At Pellegrini she established "wine tasting 101" in which the "students" were given various food products such as lychee nuts to smell and taste, thereby learning the aromas commonly used to describe wine. This event was a success and led to other food and wine experiences.

Keri moved on to Martha Clara, where she worked in marketing and event planning. She is now marketing director at Duck Walk Vineyards North, where weddings, fund raisers, and the wine club are the major emphasis.

Over the years the wineries have grown into entertainment centers and weekend destinations for many people They have also become venues for cultural events that have enriched our lives. In reality they are businesses like any other with lots of bills to pay, but they also play a large part in serving the community.

Jo-Ann Perry

Jo-Ann Perry is a pioneer in the winery tour business on the North Fork. She founded Vintage Tours in 1997 and, although she has intentionally kept it small, the business is highly respected by customers and wineries alike and is an example of how target marketing and hard work can succeed on the North Fork. Groups are now a big part of tasting room business due to successful marketing and the strongly enforced laws on drunk driving. Limousines,

Jo-Ann Perry

vans, and buses blanket the area on weekends carrying corporate groups, church groups, college friends, and of course bachelor and bachelorette parties. The various companies that organize the tours have developed reputations that vary across the whole spectrum of behavior. The wineries welcome some groups more than others.

From 1981 to 1986, Jo-Ann was working as a travel agent in Hawaii, and she would introduce tourists to a local person who would drive them around the area for a day, acquainting them with the sights and activities that they could pursue during their stay. People loved getting the "inside story" from one who knew. Jo-Ann returned to Long Island in 1986 and settled down in her home town of Peconic. Her husband Tom started the first Chem-Dry Franchise in Suffolk County and she helped him out while bringing up their children. But she took a weekend job at Pindar Winery in 1992 where she worked the tasting room and became one of the tour guides trained by Dr. Damianos and Jane Utz. During the next five years Jo-Ann became knowledgeable in the fine points of winemaking and wine tasting, information that became valuable later on.

It was in 1997 that Jo-Ann's husband Tom found a van at Lucas Ford in Southold that sat 15 people, was for sale at a great price, and even had a purple color resembling red wine grapes. This was all it took for Jo-Ann to found Vintage Tours. She began by focusing on the marinas in the area, because the boaters usually didn't have cars and the taxi service in our area was almost non-

existent. She would pick up people, usually couples, and tour them around the North Fork, talking as she went. They would visit four local wineries and stop at a local restaurant for lunch. The whole trip would take five hours and cost $35 per

person. Along the way they would be able to taste the wines, meet new people, and learn new things about our region.

Year after year, Vintage Tours has prospered, but Jo-Ann has kept it small and stuck to the same format. Today, she uses a website extensively and draws many customers from the B&B's that have proliferated on the North Fork. She now has a beautiful new custom van and provides box lunches prepared by a local restaurant. She still visits four wineries on each trip, but the cost has risen to $75 per person.

Because of her knowledge and excellent reputation with the wineries, Jo-Ann is given special treatment by most owners and her groups are rarely refused. She also specializes in going to small artisanal wineries that are off the beaten path. Her schedule is flexible and not announced ahead of time, allowing her to adjust as necessary to prevailing conditions. The only problem is that her van is usually sold out far in advance on busy weekends in the summer and fall seasons.

Jo-Ann Perry is a hard-working person who has built a successful business on the North Fork. With her bright personality, winery knowledge, and the sincere wish to make people happy, she has become a great asset to our wine community.

THE WHOLESALE REPRESENTATIVE

Tom Morgan

Since 1976, when the first vintage of Long Island wine was released, retail liquor stores and restaurants around the region and in Manhattan have been a tough sell. They just didn't latch on to local wine the way that many of us thought they would. The reasons are elusive and complex: wine shop clerks will suggest wine that is popular, not choosing to stick their neck out; sommeliers in fine dining restaurants like what a more expensive wine does for their check average; and customers are drawn in by exotic, out-of-town labels. And now — 32 years later — not much has changed. But one person has convinced owners of package stores and restaurants that Lenz makes exceptional wine that can stand alongside any wine in the world. He has also backed up that claim with personal service that treats a customer with intelligence and respect. That person is Thomas Owen

Tom Morgan

Morgan, who has been the wholesale manager for Lenz Winery for the past 22 years. His philosophy is to quietly create Lenz customers "one person at a time".

Tom was born in Rockville Centre in 1944. He went to Oceanside High School, graduating in 1962. He earned his bachelor's degree in English from Union College in Schenectady in 1966 and then spent a year in law school. This was followed by joining the Coast Guard Reserve and spending a few years in an unsatisfying job in a sales position with a paper company. But during this time Tom was learning about wine and drinking wine along with many other Americans in the early 1970's. He finally called on a New York area distributor, Star Industries, and asked them for a job. He was hired as a sales representative in 1974 and eventually became the wine manager for all three divisions of the company. This experience allowed Tom to become acquainted with the important wine shop proprietors from Sherry-Lehman, Zachy's, and Sokolin in the city and Pop's, Post Liquors, and Amagansett Wines on the Island. He went on to work for Charles LeFranc, the distributor of Chateau Petrus, and National Distributors, where he sold Bordeaux futures. It was now 1986.

At an exclusive wine tasting in the city, called "View From the Vineyard," Tom was to meet Peter Lenz. Peter was a tall, imposing man of German origin who looked like a German prince. His wife Pat was a chef from Westhampton. The two of them had run a stunning restaurant called The Moveable Feast until they created Lenz Winery in 1978. Tom Morgan joined them in 1986 and has remained with Lenz ever since. After Peter Carroll bought the winery in 1988, Tom continued on as wholesale manager and became part of a long lasting team, along with winemaker Eric Fry and vineyard manager Sam McCullough.

Tom knew that by the 1993 vintage, Lenz was producing world-class wine. Their Merlot was elegant, with beautifully balanced fruit, acidity, and alcohol. Its tannins were soft enough for consumption now, but you knew that it had the structure to last for a long time. The only problem was to get others exposed to the wine and to help them get over deep prejudices and old habits. Long Island wines were often perceived as pricey and not up to the standards of the famous labels. So Tom Morgan suggested a marketing campaign similar to the Pepsi challenge of the time. He and owner Peter Carroll devised a series of blind tastings beginning out east (at Ross' North Fork Restaurant) and ending in Manhattan. Serious wine people were asked to be judges and the scoring was carefully controlled. Famous wines such as Chateau Lafitte and Chateau Petrus were placed in the same flights as Lenz Merlot. And every time, Lenz Merlot scored very high, often beating out these celebrated brands. The marketing that followed these tastings has done much to focus attention on the high quality of Long Island wine in general.

Tom Morgan feels that a solution to the problem of having to depend on unreliable clerks and sommeliers to sell quality wine is to do it through subscription. The customer is won over by tasting the wine at the winery, or perhaps at an event such as a wine dinner at a restaurant. He or she then joins the wine club and is guaranteed preferential treatment. Lenz has taken the unusual step of saving its finest wines for wine club members and restaurants. This rewards the loyal customer and guarantees wine for them, even in off years when the best wines may not be made. The long career of Tom highlights the many challenges that our wines have in gaining wide acceptance by a skeptical public. He has done much to meet that challenge.

Peggy Lauber

Peggy Lauber has been a winery owner and winery employee. She has also been a sales representative for New York importers and distributors of wines from around the world. Her experience on both sides of the fence, and with a wide variety of both Long Island and imported wines, has given her a unique perspective on the wholesale market.

Where Long Island wines are sold, the sales "mix" for any winery is a very important market-  ing decision. In the early days, many people thought that retail liquor stores and wine shops throughout Suffolk and Nassau counties would embrace the idea of selling the new Long Island wines. We also pictured the restaurants and wine shops of Manhattan selling our wine. But it just didn't happen — at least not in the way we thought it would. So, gradually over the years most wineries on the East

Peggy Lauber

End have expanded their tasting rooms and relied on a much higher percentage of sales from them. The strategy has worked and has contributed to the destination status of the North Fork. The only problem is the danger of blurring the line between quality wine and entertainment.

Peggy Lauber understands the importance of the broader marketplace. You want a beautiful tasting room adjoining the winery and vineyards. A special ambiance is created by the yeasty smell of wine production, the beauty of the grape vines, and the enjoyment of being in the country. It is also the perfect place to sell the more expensive wines, which often end up as gifts or at a special occasion meal. But we also want our wines showcased on the shelves of wine stores, the tables of restaurants and hotels — and ultimately on the everyday dinner table of consumers.

Peggy feels that the ideal marketing mix is one-third of sales from the tasting room (including wine club); one-third from direct wholesale (this usually means that the East End community is served by your own employee); and one-third from a wholesale distributor. At her present job at Wolffer Estate vineyard, Peggy is the sales manager and Winebow is the distributor. But what is critical to make this formula work is quality wine at a reasonable price. She identifies this price range as $18-$25 retail. This is a little more than the heavily marketed mass production brands and less than most famous world class wines. But a quality wine at this price will sell and attract repeat business. There is just no place for those overweight fancy bottles of ego-driven expensive wine in the wholesale marketplace.

Peggy Lauber was born in Highland Park, Illinois in 1953 and came east to go to college at Skidmore in Saratoga Springs, New York. She graduated with a degree in English in 1975 and took a job in New York city at an ad agency that specialized in pharmaceuticals. It was there that she met her future husband Joel Lauber and they were married in 1980. They were introduced by a friend to the North Fork and ended up buying a small house in Orient as a weekend getaway.

By 1992 Peggy and Joel were having marital problems and a counselor advised "doing something together" like starting a small business on the North Fork. They bought about 30 acres of land that was partially planted in vineyards in 1993. They renamed it Corey Creek Vineyards. It didn't save their marriage, but it did produce an outstanding batch of Chardonnay grapes. Dan Kleck, the winemaker at Palmer, made the wine which they labeled Corey Creek Chardonnay.

Their timing could not have been better. The '93 vintage was excellent, as were the '94 and '95. Without a tasting room or distributor, Peggy went around selling the wine out of the trunk of her car. With a little help from wine writer Howard Goldberg (and others), the wine was a big hit. Even though Peggy and Joel had separated by now, they felt they must go on to develop this wine business, and in 1997 they got architect Elizabeth Thompson to transform their old potato barn into a beautiful tasting room overlooking their vineyard.

In 1999 the Laubers sold their vineyard and tasting room to Michael Lynne, who went on to purchase Bedell Cellars the following year. For them it was a stressful decision because the young winery was so successful, but they didn't feel that they had the resources to take it to the next level. Joel and Peggy were divorced and Peggy became a sales representative, first for Victor Schwartz; later she became the East end sales rep for Winebow. This is where Peggy moved from her love affair with Long Island wine to selling prestigious labels from around the world. Her heart was with Long Island, but sometimes the soap opera side of it was troubling.

In 2001, Michael Lynne approached her with a lucrative offer to come back and be the sales manager for Corey Creek and Bedell Cellars. With some reluctance, she accepted the position and remained there for the next four years. It finally became too difficult and she went back to the international scene with a job at Billington Imports. This lasted one year before she ended up at her present job with Wolffer Estates. Peggy feels strongly that Long Island wines can compete in the world marketplace. She also believes that we have to concentrate on mid-level quality wine and "get real" about pricing. It sounds like pretty good advice.

IN 2009, WINERY GROWTH CONTINUES ON THE NORTH FORK

Though the proliferation of wineries has slowed from the boom-ing days of the late 1990's, growth has continued and has often led in different directions. The actual acreage planted still hovers around 3000, but is divided up in different ways.

Much expansion has happened in the small artisanal winery that produces less than 2000 cases of wine annually. These small family operations have contributed some very good quality wine and lots of personality to the region. But we have also seen growth in some larger operations that include production facilities, tast-ing rooms, and vineyards. The following wineries are examples of this growth. At press time, some are still in the final stages of construction.

Jason Damianos and Jason's Vineyard

Jason is the first of the "second generation" of wine people to open his own winery. It seems fitting since he is the son of Dr. Herodotus Damianos, owner of the oldest winery on Long Island under continuous family manage-ment. But unlike Pindar or Duck Walk, Jason"s vineyard is a small artisanal operation built on 20 acres of land in Jamesport. He purchased the property back in 1996 and planted 15 acres of vines, using the close spacing that he learned while studying at the University of Bordeaux. The grape varieties include Caber-

Jason Damianos

net Sauvignon, Cabernet Franc, Merlot, malbec, and Chardonnay.

Jason predicts that production will be about 4000 cases of wine per year, to will be sold exclusively at the winery.

The winery is a beautiful two-story building that has a replica of an ancient Greek and Roman warship, called a trireme, as its centerpiece. Triremes were long vessels with three rows of oars on each side. First developed by the Phoenicians, they are best known from the fleets of ancient Greece, and were the dominant warship in the Mediterranean from the 7th to 4th centuries B.C.

Jason's Vineyard – Jamesport

The ship actually serves as the winery's tasting bar. Upstairs is a private function room with an open display kitchen and an outside deck overlooking the vineyard. The whole building has a rustic look with its rough-hewn wooden floors. There is an underground barrel aging room with tunnels connecting it to the crush pad and storage areas.

It seems that Jason's long experience in the wine business and his family's heritage is reflected in the design of his winery.

Tom and Cynthia Rosicki

The story of Tom and Cynthia Rosicki and their new winery, Sparkling Pointe, sounds too romantic to be true: they met at a debutante

Tom and Cynthia Rosicki

ball at the Waldorf Astoria over a glass of Champagne; they were married shortly after and honeymooned on a boat in Chesapeake Bay accompanied by numerous bottles of sparkling wine; and now, 20 years later, they are opening a winery dedicated solely to sparkling wine. They are still having fun and hope to share the romance of sparkling wine with others.

Tom is a former FBI agent, and both he and Cynthia are successful attorneys, partners in the Plainview law firm of Rosicki, Rosicki and Associates. They are as passionate in their support of people challenged with disabilities as they are about sparkling wine.

After coming out to the North Fork for a long time to visit Cynthia's parents, they purchased a 12-acre piece of land (the former Aksin Nursery) across from Mudd Vineyards on Route 48 in Southold. When asked by Steve Mudd what they wanted to plant in the new vineyard they told him they didn't know. But when Steve asked them what they liked to drink, they both answered, "Champagne!" So the decision was made to plant Chardonnay, Pinot Noir, and Pinot meuniere — the traditional grapes of the Champagne region in France. When it came time to choose a winemaker they chose Gilles Martin, a local winemaker who comes from and was trained in Champagne. Until the winery is completed, they continue to make their wine at Premium Wine Group in Mattituck. Their new winery, tasting room, and visitor center is being designed by Nancy Steelman and will open in 2009.

The process for making quality wine in the traditional *Methode Champenoise* method is time-consuming, labor-intensive, and requires a skilled winemaker, thus making the wine expensive. First the grapes are harvested, run through a crusher-destemmer, and gently pressed into clear grape juice before entering the stainless fermentation tank. If the wine is made entirely with the Chardonnay grape, the finished sparkling wine is usually called "Blanc de Blanc." If the wine is made entirely from the Pinot Noir grape, the resulting product would usually be called "Blanc de Noir." Much of the time, sparkling wine is made from blends, including wines from different vintages. That is why most sparkling wine does not have a vintage date on the bottle. In this way a consistent style can be maintained from vintage to vintage.

After the wine is fermented it is blended and a mixture of sugar and yeast is added to create the second fermentation. This is called "liqueur de tirage" and is done while the wine is still in the tank. It is then put into the bottles and capped. These bottles are placed on their sides in a cool cellar and the second fermentation takes place in the bottle. The carbon dioxide is trapped in the bottle and the sugar is converted to alcohol, resulting in a completely dry wine. This process only takes a couple of weeks, but the bottles are left to age with the dead yeast cells (or lees) still in the bottle. Quality wines will rest this way for 12 months and up to 6 years and more for some very special wines. The time of this lees contact determines the style and character of the finished wine. As this time increases, the bubbles become smaller and the carbon dioxide releases itself more slowly when the bottle is opened. With age, the decomposing yeast cells create a "toasty" aroma, and the fruit flavors become more complex.

After this second bottle-fermentation and aging is complete, the wine is subjected to a process called "remuage" or riddling. The dead yeast particles are loosened and maneuvered to the top of the bottle. The neck of the bottle is then frozen and a small quantity of wine pops out along with the dead yeast cells. This is called "degorgement" or disgorging. While the bottle is still open a small amount of wine is added to top it off. This may or may not contain a small amount of sugar, depending on the final taste profile desired. This process is called "dosage." Some of the classical terms used for sparkling wine sweetness profiles are "Extra Brut" — no sugar; "Brut" — a tiny dosage; "Sec" — medium sweet; and "Demi-Sec" — sweet. After resting for another three to six months the bottles are ready to be labeled and sold. It's important to know that once a bottle of sparkling wine is finally released it is ready to drink and, unlike some still wines, does not improve further with more age.

You can see that producing quality sparkling wine is a complex process that requires time and patience. You can also see that the romance of making this wine is almost as great as the romance of drinking it.

Clovis Point

Clovis Point Vineyards was founded as a small vineyard on the Main Road in Jamesport in 2001. In 2007, principal partners Nasrallah Misk and Hal Ginsburg converted a 1920's barn into a beautiful tasting room. They are now growing Merlot, Cabernet Franc, Cabernet Sauvignon, syrah, and Chardonnay on 20 acres of land surrounding the tasting room. The modest size of this operation seems to be a continuing trend in new winery development. Perhaps the tight quality control and the fact that most of the sales occur in the tasting room offsets the advantages of large volume.

Carmela Paciullo

Clovis Point Winery

Carmela Paciullo, a tasting room veteran on the North Fork, is their general manager. She has worked at Pellegrini, Laurel Lake, Gallucio, and Osprey's Dominion. She also spent three years as a wholesale rep for the prestigious wine distributor, Lauber Imports. With her outgoing personality, rich wine experience, and sincere customer service, Carmela has built a following for the wines of Clovis Point. Their 400 loyal wine club members are introduced to new releases, given sharp discounts, and treated to special functions at the winery.

John Leo is the winemaker and the wine is currently made at Premium Wine Group in Mattituck. The vineyard consultant is Peter Gristina. They currently produce about 3000 cases per year. The other partners are Mary Bayno, John and Renae Pine, and Richard Frey.

Steven Bate and the Long Island Wine Council

In 1981, Dave Mudd founded the Long Island Grape Growers Association as the first industry group to address the common problems of vineyard owners and managers. By 1989 this group had evolved into the Long Island Wine Council. The membership in the LIWC was restricted to owners of wineries, with associate memberships available for vineyard owners and people in the trade. Its mission is "to obtain recognition for Long Island Wine Country as a premium wine-producing region, and to provide a coordinated effort for the promotion and development of the region's wine industry." Phil Nugent was hired as a part time director, with the mission of promoting the new industry. Jane Baxter Lynn became the first full-time LIWC director, gaining recognition as a promoter of our region by overseeing the annual barrel tastings and Windows on Long Island events. When she left in 2004 to pursue other interests, Steven Bate was hired as her replacement. He remains as director of the wine council today.

Steven Bate was born in New York and grew up in Riverside, Connecticut, graduating from Greenwich High School. An avid skier, Steve became the Connecticut high school ski champion in 1976. He went on to St. Lawrence University, where he majored in government and was a member of the school's Division I ski team. After graduating in 1980, he worked as a paralegal and then as consumer correspondent for Cuisinarts before heading to

Columbia for graduate school, where he received two degrees, a Master of International Affairs in 1984 and an MBA in 1986.

While working for Coopers and Lybrand as an international tax consultant, Steve happened upon tickets to the trade-only Vinexpo in Bordeaux, France. By some luck and coincidence he parlayed that trip into a job with the OECD, where he

Steven Bate

worked on the business advisory committee as an advisor on a range of policy issues. He worked and lived in Paris for the next 12 years. Steve's personal interest in wine motivated him to visit all of the wine producing regions of France and several other wine regions around Europe during this period. In 2004 he was ready for a change, and answered a classified ad seeking a new director for the wine council on Long Island.

The wine council has grown to over 40 members and in 2008 had an annual budget of about $400,000. About a third of this budget came from dues, with the rest coming from a combination of grants and winery- or sponsor-matching contributions for specific projects. Steve Bate says that "in 2008 the wine council spent some $300,000 on marketing, which covers both our efforts to generate consumer/trade interest and our activities to attract tourism to the region — specifically to wine tasting rooms.

Steve writes, "Beyond the ongoing effort to increase coverage of our region in both specialist and general-interest media, we take a strategic approach to coordinating regional event participation, more recently with an emphasis on the New York City metropolitan area, but also locally, with the sponsorship of the Stony Brook conference and our efforts to develop regional tourism through projects such as the Jazz on the Vine promotion. We also produce and distribute promotional materials such as our Touring Guide/Map and maintain our regional website. Drawing on my previous background, we also provide advice on policy issues affecting the wine industry, but always in close cooperation with Joe Gergela and the LIFB, who does such an outstanding job of looking out for all LI agricultural interests in Albany."

Because each winery differs greatly in size, production, and marketing direction, coming up with a consensus of how to best promote our region is a very difficult task. The owners are a group of interesting individuals who have strong personalities and very different needs. Steven Bate has kept a low profile, working behind the scenes to make the system go, and to keep all the wine council members happy while making the right decisions for the region as a whole.

A LITTLE HUMOR LIGHTENS UP A SERIOUS INDUSTRY

Michael Todd

When we start discussing wine the conversation often gets technical very quickly. Grape variety, blending, vintage, oak aged, malolactic fermentation, food matches, price, etc. We forget that the enjoyment of wine is a very subjective experience, and each bottle of quality wine is full of stories and often charged with emotion. That's the real beauty of wine. It's much more than 750ml of fermented grape juice. It's about the people who made it, the town it was made in, and the journey it traveled to get to our table. And lest we start taking ourselves too seriously, there is room for a little humor in that bottle.

The late Michael Todd supplied that humor along with much more in his publication, *The GrapeZine*. Michael was a British-born freelance art director, graphic designer, and consultant to the New York Times among other things. He and his wife Claudia Payne had a summer house in Sag Harbor which became the headquarters for the "Zine." The first issue came out in 1993. It was outrageous in its descriptions of people and very funny. Michael described it as the "Eccentric and Essential Guide to East End Food and Wine." And that it was. Winemakers, chefs, and almost everyone else, including owners, were talked about and made fun of. It was the first time that

Michael Todd

any publication had focused on the people behind the scenes in the wine industry. As a local chef, I found myself and many of my colleagues in his magazine repeatedly. He told the world about us and also showed in a very graphic and humorous way the link between food and wine. The Zine also had honest ratings of many local wines and the restaurants that served them, but they weren't boring or pompous. Michael Todd personally visited tasting rooms and restaurants, and attended many wine related events. He had the guts to say when something wasn't good or to make fun of sacred cows, but he was probably the best ambassador we ever had. He certainly drew much-needed attention to our growing industry and the people who surrounded it. Michael Todd passed away after a brief illness in 1998 at the age of 51. After six years and fifty-three issues, *The GrapeZine* died along with him.

The GrapeZine was indeed outrageous. A picture on the cover of one issue had winery owner Dr. Damianos riding a duck with the caption "Quack! No, He's a Doctor." This headline announced the Doctor's purchase of Southampton Winery and his decision to call it Duck Walk Vineyards. With magazine sections called "So, What?" and "Rumors, Lies, and Innuendo," you had to laugh. The GrapeZine always began with Michael's column called "My Bit." In his August 12, 1998 issue he said "...And though, throughout these past six years, I have been a thorn in the flesh of several of the individual winery owners (specifically) and of the collective (if that's the word) Long Island Wine Council in general, I don't think any of them would deny that the GrapeZine has, both directly and indirectly, had a more significant effect on both their current public visibility and the booming sales of their wines than any other single factor..."

After his death, this quote from a November 1996 edition of the "Zine" proved prophetic: "Two weeks after he reportedly vaporized while sitting at his computer, *GrapeZine* publisher Michael Todd was today officially declared 'Lost in Cyberspace.' Todd, whose rancorous musings on the subject of wine were frequently dismissed by critics as petty eno-babble, had recently been attempting to develop 'a major new outernet communications concept' known as Wine Intelligence Netcom Optimization, or WINO.

On Wednesday, Todd's computer and printer (a rare 1995 model), the sole extent of his publishing 'empire,' will be cremated in a long-abandoned black Jaguar in the dead vineyard of the former Bridgehampton Winery. A funeral procession, led by a twenty-mule team, will march twice around the Sag Dump and down the turnpike to the final resting place. The cremation is to be ignited with a 12-liter bottle of Lemberger grappa, and the ceremony will feature a requiem interruptus hummed by the British Belching Baritone Bartender's Choir. A funeral toast will follow with the opening of 'several fresh LI Graves.' Todd is survived by a nine-bottle wine collection, some multicolored sandals, five faded black t-shirts and a vintage Chrysler. In lieu of flowers, mourners are asked to send donations to their local chapter of the Society for the Prevention of Mad Dogs and Englishmen."

Michael Todd's "ambassador" and partner Howard Dickerson assembled a tribute to him from which this quote was taken. A memorial scholarship was set up for Michael at Suffolk Community College to be offered to a student enrolled in wine industry-related courses. I was present at a memorial service held at Chef Todd Jacob's restaurant, Tierra Mar. Michael Todd and *The GrapeZine* have been sorely missed in the decade since his death. Sometimes we just need someone to help us lighten up.

Howard Dickerson

Howard is the son of successful North Fork potato farmers, Parker and Betsy Dickerson. As vines replaced potatoes and cauliflower as the crops of choice, very few traditional farmers switched to viticulture. Howard is one who made the transition to the new industry. He is a little eccentric, with a love of wine, history, culture, and agriculture. He also loves to philosophize and to laugh. I don't know how to categorize him other than to call him one of the "loose cannons" of the Long Island wine industry.

Howard graduated from Southold High School in 1975 and went to Cornell University as an

Howard Dickerson

agricultural engineering student. After two years, he left and took a job as a technician working with Bill Sanok at the Cornell Research Lab in Baiting Hollow. They were just starting to work with vinifera grapes. In 1978, Howard went to the Hargrave Vineyard and met Alex and Louisa for the first time. Shortly after, in 1980, he went back to school at the University of Nebraska, where he was a liberal arts major. He graduated in 1983 and came back to the family farm in Southold.

Howard's first business venture was growing lettuce and microgreens in a hydroponic greenhouse. This worked pretty well at first and Howard bought a truck to deliver his product. It seemed like a great idea to be able to get fresh, local produce even during the winter. But the greens lacked a wide customer base and the costs of heating the greenhouse was astronomical. By the late 1980's national brands of specialty produce were growing and the competition became intense. Howard's business crashed and all that was left was the truck.

The local wine industry was expanding greatly in the early 1990's, and Howard's next venture was a wine delivery service. After all, he already had the truck. For a commission or a flat fee he would deliver cases of local wine to New York City destinations and others throughout Nassau and Suffolk counties. Initially it was a big success and by 1995 Howard had three trucks on the road with people to drive them. But by 1998 many of the wineries were taking on wholesale distributors to market their wines in the metro area. A delivery service was no longer needed and Howard was out of luck again.

In 1992 Howard became friends with Pindar winemaker Bob Henn. This led to his getting involved in vineyard installation, vineyard management, and growing nursery stock grapevines — including grafting. He went on to help plant many local vineyards, but was not able to find a permanent home with any of the wineries. In 1994, Howard took another about-face and joined Michael Todd with his new publication, *The GrapeZine*. Finally he had found a soulmate and someone as crazy as himself. They got along great together as Howard became known as "Ze Ambassador" to the wine people. He wrote and edited many articles, along with numerous other duties. But tragedy occurred when Michael died suddenly in 1998, and *The GrapeZine* was gone.

Howard Dickerson really has been a great "Ambassador" for the Long Island wine industry. He is intelligent and knowledgeable as he spreads the good word about our wines and the people who make them. With his engaging personality and bright outlook he is a pleasure to be around. He himself admits that he doesn't respond to authority well and he is not willing to follow someone else's path. He is a truly independent soul.

GrapeZine Humor

Tales from the Tasting Rooms
by Gwendolen Groocock and David Goldman
(The GrapeZine, August 1994)

"Do you have any Carbonnay?" "I'm really looking for a dry-sweet wine...." "Where are the bathrooms?" Along with endless heavy cases of wine, these utterings are just part of the burden that the long-suffering staffs of the East End wineries' tasting rooms must bear.

These charming, bright, and unnerringly polite people are the unsung heroes of our wine industry. Not for them the glory, recognition, and pecuniary recompense bestowed upon the owners and winemakers. They are merely the vital link, the contact with the visiting public, the ones who sell the damn stuff!

Every day after day these brave foot soldiers of Bacchus must with patience and a straight face handle the foibles and foolishness of often demanding, occasionally rude, and sometimes wonderfully weird customers. Stories abound that are humorous, outrageous, and that sometimes border on the unbelievable.

Cynthia Fuller, now at Paumanok Vineyards, recalls one very elegant lady visitor with a less than tactful turn of phrase: "She had tasted a number of our wines without much comment," says Cynthia, "Then we served her our dessert wine. She closed her eyes and stated, in a very loud voice, "This is the most delicious thing you could put in your mouth..."

On a similarly tasteful note, the romantic atmosphere of

the wineries did inspire one imaginative suitor to orchestrate his proposal of marriage in the barrel cellar at Pindar Vineyards, complete with candlelight and Champagne.

While most of the tasting room staff we know could find little lascivious about their work places, that hasn't stopped more adventurous visitors from engaging in, shall we say, amorous behavior. Furious necking sessions in winery tasting rooms, during guided tours, or in parking lots are not uncommon.

For at least one couple, though, a kiss was not enough. During the Chardonnay Classic at Bridgehampton Winery, they were discovered, well, in flagrante delicto, among the fermentation tanks by a tasting room staffer. The lure of all that gleaming, chilly stainless steel must have proved irresistible!

While wineries have inspired desire in some, it brings out the artist in others. C. Michael Jones, now General Manager at Pellegrini, recalled one interesting would-be performer: "This guy came in with his bicycle helmet on and started tasting," he said, "When he'd tasted a few, he just suddenly burst into song. I think it was the soundtrack from some movie (Days of Wine and Roses?) His impromtu aria completed, the singer departed. "The worst thing was that he did't even have a voice," Jones noted.

But he can't have been as tone deaf as the toothless songstress who regaled her fellow Hell's Angels in the Pindar tasting room late one February afternoon.

Staff also find themselves answering questions on everything from where to eat or sleep on the East End to how to start a stalled car. Sometimes the information requested reveals a startling lack of geographical knowledge. More than one confused client has asked for the quickest route south from Southold to Southampton, and has been amazed to discover that the journey involves travel by sea.

Susan Skrezek, Palmer Vineyards tasting room manager, recalls a phone call from one potential visitor: "The woman wanted to know how long it would take her to walk from the nearest train station to Palmer," she says, "When I told her it might be an hour or two, she was a little surprised."

We recall these incidents fondly, for they are just a very small fraction of our daily public, and they certainly serve to lighten the day. While tasting room staff around the East End still find many customers are less than cognizant of wine in general or of Long Island wines in particular, all agree that this is changing, if slowly, and that the most rewarding part of their job is to educate those interested enough to take the trouble to visit.

As Susan Skrezek says, "We seem to be getting more and more people these days who are more knowledgeable about wine, and what's even nicer is that they have come to see us, to taste Long Island wines specifically."

See you over the counter.

The following article from the August 1998 *GrapeZine* is a parody of Alex and Louisa Hargrave in their search for the perfect place to grow grapes:

Long Island's Hot Potatoes?! You Betcha!
special to the New Fork Tines, Cutchogue, NY: August 10, 2023

Twenty-five years ago, in 1998, Aleksander and Loislava Hrgrovszki, from Poland, were visiting the North Fork of Long Island, when the idea hit them. They had been visiting relatives in nearby Riverhead — a wedding of mutual cousins — more or less on vacation, glad to get away for a few days from the problem that had been nagging at both their minds for some time. They knew that the days were slipping by fast and soon they would have to return to Warsaw. Once back in Poland they would have to admit defeat, or compromise their principles. Aleksander was the youngest son of a Polish farmer. His father had risen to prominence under Communist chief General Jaruszelski, increasing his landholdings as the Party rewarded his loyalty and support with grants of additional acreage. Stanislas Hrgrovski was known as the potato Baron of Lodz. Aleks' wife, Loislava, was the grandaughter of a Party apparatchik, a party hack who had distinguished himself by being among the first to applaud the Soviet Union's "counter-revolutionary" actions in Hungary in 1956 and Czechoslovakia in 1968.

Aleksander and Loislava were childhood friends who had grown up as privileged members of Poland's Communist Party elite, marrying shortly before the collapse of the Soviet Union. After the fall of the Iron Curtain, their futures had been far from secure. Providentially, Aleksander's parents had set up a U.S. dollar account with Banque Pictet in Geneva, in which they had managed to salt away some money "for a rainy day." "The Party's over, thanks to that rabblerouser, Lech Walesa, and his comrade-in-arms, Karol Wojtila," Stash had told his son. His father told Aleksander that he would let him have enough money to start a business. Aleks and Loislava had initially had no idea what to do. They had never really had to make a decision before. Both were more or less professional students. Aleks had studied Political Philosophy at the University of Warsaw in Poland, and he had a Masters degree in Dialectical Linguistics from the Patrice Lumumba University in Moscow.

He toyed with the idea of farming, but his father cast a big shadow. Loislava, however, had developed an interest in ecology (that would have been frowned upon in the old days). She had come across an old text in her father-in-law's library, listing all the old varieties of potato that had been grown in Poland before Stalin collectivized all Soviet farms and Khruschev enforced a potato monoculture designed to drive farm output up to meet the five year plan. That textbook was the spark that finally sent Aleks and Loislava off in a definite direction: they would start a potato farm and rehabilitate all the heirloom varieties that had vanished from Polish agriculture.

But where? They researched horticulture textbooks on potatoes. Then they traveled far and wide, initially within Poland, and then farther and farther afield, in the foothills of the Carpathian mountains, in Hungary, in Serbia, along the Danube; as far east as the Pripet marshes and as far south as the plain of Edirne on the Turkish border. They just couldn't find the right combination. They needed a light, sandy soil, slightly loamy, that would drain well, with a late spring, good sunshine, steady rainfall, and plenty of groundwater to provide irrigation in times of temporary drought. After their protected upbringing, they weren't used to hard work and the search for a perfect spot was exhausting.

When the invitation to travel to the United States for a cousin's wedding first arrived, in the spring of 1998, their first instinct had been not to go. They were still deeply suspicious of that decadent country, their implacable foe throughout the cold war years. They half-believed all the old propaganda, and they were even more annoyed at the thought of Americans crowing over the eventual outcome. But in the end they went. It would give them a break from the fruitless search for the perfect potato farm.

In Riverhead, they had been pleasantly surprised. The town looked like some of the nicer small towns in western Poland, near the border with the old Democratic Republic. The wedding was a joyous occasion and they caught up with members of branches of the family who had made their way to America, by one means or another, over the years.

Their hosts showed them around Long Island. One day they visited "the Hamptons." But Aleksander and Loislava were not as gullible as their relatives. They were supposed to believe that this was how Americans really lived?! Every other car was a Mercedes, a Porsche, or a Range Rover! The restaurants were always crowded and there were so many of them! The clothes people were wearing were the kind people wear in the movies — American movies! And the houses. The people who rented them for three months in the summer were paying ridiculous sums. For that much money, back in Poland, you could buy a whole town! No! Clearly this was a Potemkin village. A CIA front inhabited by actors to impress visitors from the east. They would not be fooled.

Another day turned out to be fateful. Two cousins said they would take them on a tour of the local wineries on the North Fork. They drove east from Riverhead on Route 25, stopping at Pellegrini, Bedell, and Lenz. Their cousins raved about the wines, but Aleks and Loislava didn't like them at all. They were too rich, too opulent, almost cloying. Here was the decadent side of American life.

Their visit to America was coming to an end. They would be glad to get back, though, all-in-all, it had been a good trip. A break from their urgent search in Europe and a relief to find that America wasn't the paradise-on-earth they had secretly feared it might prove to be.

On the way back to Riverhead they swung north onto Route 48 and stopped at one last winery. As they stood sipping the wine ("This was more like it," thought Aleksander, "My uncle used to make wine like this from the grapes on his back porch. Really grapey, with a bite in the back.") Aleksander looked out idly over the rows of dilapidated vineyards. He was thinking about the journey home when his eye fell on a For Sale sign. In the background, a tour guide was talking about the winery. The words went in one ear and out the other. "...210 days in the growing season...deep, well-drained sandy, loamy soil...And so the leaves are the sails that bring the ship into harbor...The carpenter of the vine is the architect of the wine...." He read the sign: FOR SALE, 65 ACRE FARM — 15 ACRES STILL IN VINEYARDS. $3.3 MILLION WITH INVENTORY, $4.0 MILLION WITHOUT. "That's it!" he yelled, spilling the rest of his wine and turning to find Loislava. They just had enough in their secret account in Switzerland to buy this property. Of course they'd have to take the inventory to get the lower price but that was not a problem. They could always pour it down the drain! Give it to the poor! Hell, they could even drink it themselves! It really wasn't that bad! Better than the muck they'd had to pretend they liked at the other wineries! Anyway, that didn't matter! The point was — he almost shouted to Loislava — "This is the perfect place to grow potatoes! How did these people all miss it! Here they were, prancing around planting grapevines, brewing up this foul smelling muck, when right under their noses they had the best potato-growing acreage in the entire world!! To the consternation of the indignant tour guide, Loislava and Aleks danced a polka, right there in the tasting room.

A week later, after wiring all their funds from Geneva, Aleks and Loislava bought the farm, pulled out the scraggly vines and planted the entire acreage in potatoes. The rest, as they say, is history. After a year or two, the Hrgrovszkis' first crops were well reviewed by the potato cognoscenti.

The Potato Advocate said of one Drgrovszki Peruvian Inca culti-
var: "This is one of the best potatoes I have ever tasted from
outside Idaho. It offers up a moderately intense, smoky, hazel-
nut, honeyed, apple-scented nose. Full-bodied, rich and Ida-
hoan, this well-grown tightly knit, expansive, well-endowed potato
should eat well now, and improve with two to three years of
root-cellaring. It is an impressive first effort from the Hrgrovszkis.
It should eat well with chicken and other poultry, and it promises to mash, whip, and blend exquisitely."

The Potato Spectator was equally enthusiastic: "It's a styl-
ish, polite, elegant potato with a healthy pale yellow-white
color. An attractive, understated set of aromatics. Not highly
extracted or excessively powerful, this potato offers considerable charm, elegance and earthy ripe flavors in a silky-
textured format. In spite of its accessibility, it promises to
last through at least two winters. At these prices, I would
rather whip up a plate of these taters with my meat loaf than
lash out for the Grand Cru Russet Burbanks from Idaho,
which are, frankly, becoming overpriced."

The SpudZine's editor/publisher raved: "Blimey! I took
one bite of this bloody spud, served up lightly boiled with a
roast chicken and brown sauce, and my flabber was gasted.
Bugger me! I 'aven't 'ad soddin' taters like these since me
ol' Mum did 'em wiv the Sunday joint — and that was donkey's
years ago. They're great. Snap 'em up while you can."

Hrgrovszki's potato sales skyrocketed. Customers lust-
ing after new baggings were knocking on the door at 6am;
"futures" were swiftly offered, and as swiftly sold. Certain
varieties were put on strict allocation — particularly the famed
"pomme de terroir Noir." Others followed in the footsteps
of these pioneers and soon there were 1500 acres of potato
farms on the North Fork. So many people wanted to start
celebrity farms that the Town of Southold was forced to pass
legislation restricting entry. Anyone who could be proved
to have owned or rented a house anywhere in the Hamptons,
from Remsenburg to Amagansett, was ineligible to enter the
North Fork.

Now, of course, the North Fork of Long Island is an
established appellation for heirloom potato growing, and a

mecca for lovers of the noble tuber. But it was not always so. And, on this, the twenty-fifth anniversary of the rebirth of Long Island potato agriculture, we acknowledge our debt to those two hardy, indeed unlikely, pioneers: Aleksander and Loislava Hrgrovszki.

> *– Petr Cyrllskov, with additional reporting from Mikhail Tovarich.*

EPILOGUE

The personalities of the very extended "wine family" of owners, winemakers, tasting room people, marketers, vineyard workers, chefs, and others made each day a little more exciting. Like many others, I am proud to be a part of the North Fork wine community, and it is my hope that this first 35 years is only the beginning of many good vintages to come.

Knowing the wine people of the North (and South) Fork has been one of the highlights of my life. At Ross' North Fork Restaurant, we became a gathering place for many wine people and many wine events. Over the 27 years from 1973 until 2000, I enjoyed and participated in the growth of Long Island wine. Our wine list won the Wine Spectator Award of Excellence for 7 years in a row. At the 25th anniversary celebration of the Long Island wine industry, Hargrave Vineyard and Ross' Restaurant were presented with proclamations from Southold Town, Suffolk County Legislature, and New York State Assembly, and I was inducted into the Long Island Wine Council as a member emeritus.

On my sixtieth birthday, I hosted a dinner for family and friends, and we opened most of the old large format bottles of Long Island wine that I had accumulated in my cellar. There were magnums, double magnums, and even a jeraboam (six liters) of Chardonnay. The wines held up well after their years in the bottle, as did the people who made them. I wrote the following poem for this occasion:

Sixty

At first the aroma
is a little musty.

Soon nuances of cedar,
leather, and raspberries begin to emerge.

Memories come next, slowly
at first and difficult to organize.

Just as the bouquet starts to get complex,
they begin to flow.

This vintage is, according
to experts, one of the best.

But we have to judge.
Does it seem over the hill?

The tannins are very soft,
hidden behind ripe fruit and a lively acidity.

I say, a little oxidized
and beginning to get flabby.

Not true. Maturity has been reached
with great personality and character.

It will continue to develop for years to come,
revealing its mysteries.

– John Ross, July 2004

PART TWO

WINE COUNTRY
RECIPES

Cooking with Wine

Grape Varieties
and their Food Companions

COOKING WITH WINE

Wine has been used in cooking for almost as long as it has been used as a beverage. As the use of food evolved from one of sustenance to one of enjoyment, wine and other alcoholic beverages became an important part of cuisine. Fine regional cuisines naturally developed next to vineyards. Thus both France and Italy are famous for both their wine and their food. Boeuf bourguignon, coq au vin, veal Marsala, and Swiss fondue are examples of classical dishes using wine. Modern cuisine in the New World wine regions has followed this tradition in creating many local dishes that incorporate wine and spirits.

Just as good wine introduces complex aromas and flavors in the glass, it also makes food taste better when used in cooking. When we cook with wine, we use it in many ways: sometimes it is an ingredient that is added for flavor and complexity, much like an herb or spice; sometimes it is used as the cooking medium, like water or stock; sometimes it is used in a sauce to moisten a dish, making it more palatable; and sometimes it is used as a marinade to soften the fibers in meat and fish and to create new flavors in otherwise bland food.

However wine is used, a few simple rules must be followed. It is always important to cook the alcohol out of wine. If you simply add wine to a sauce or pour it on top of a dish before serving, the alcohol will have a harsh taste and totally dominate every other flavor in the dish. If the wine is reduced by boiling or cooked slowly over a period of time, the alcohol evaporates and leaves subtle flavors of fruit, oak, and yeast that can turn a simple dish into a masterpiece. The wine that is used for cooking does not have to be of the finest quality because some of its nuances will be lost in the cooking process, but it should be wine of sufficient quality to have good character after the alcohol is evaporated. Another rule is to use lighter wines in lighter foods. A light white wine is perfect for poaching a fish while a full-bodied wine is better for long, slow cooking — as in a stew. Finally, the quantity of wine in any preparation should be modest so as to complement the flavor of the dish rather than dominate it.

Wine as an Ingredient

When wine is used as an ingredient in a recipe it creates complexity and complements the other ingredients. The acidity of the wine offsets the fat in the dish and contributes to tenderness. Wine blends in with the natural juices, herbs, and vegetables to add a new demension. The most effective use of wine in cooking is with the classic braised dishes. Over time the wine is absorbed into the sauce, losing its identity, but creating new and more complex flavors.

Beef Bourguignon

Ingredients	Amounts
Beef chuck, cut in 2" chunks	4 lbs.
Salt pork, diced	8 oz.
White boiling onions	1 lb.
Butter	1 tbsp.
Carrots, coarsely chopped	1 cup
Shallots, minced	½ cup
Garlic, minced	2 tbsp.
Flour	¼ cup
Red wine	3 cups
Beef broth	1 cup
Tomato paste	1 tbsp.
Leek, white part, sliced	1 leek
Parsley stems	6
Bay leaf	1
Thyme	3 sprigs
Black pepper	1 tsp.
Mushrooms	1 lb.
Parsley, chopped	½ cup

Procedure

1. Bring 1 quart of water to a boil and blanch white onions for 2 minutes. Remove with a slotted spoon and blanch diced salt pork in the same water. Drain and dry salt pork on a paper towel. Peel onions with a small knife.

2. Melt butter in a heavy casserole or Dutch oven and add salt pork. Remove salt pork when brown and add white onions. When they are golden brown remove and set aside.

3. Turn heat to high and brown meat in batches, being careful not to crowd it in the pan. Remove and set aside.

4. Add another tbsp. of butter if necessary. Add to drippings the carrots, shallots, and garlic. Cook briefly and stir in the flour to make a roux. Cook until lightly browned.

5. Add the wine, beef broth, and tomato paste. Simmer until lightly thickened and add back the meat. Tie the leek, parsley stems, bay leaf, and thyme into a bundle with string and add to pot.

6. Add back the browned salt pork and black pepper. Bring to a boil on the stove, cover, and put into a 300 degree oven. Cook 1 hour and add the browned onions. Continue cooking until meat is very tender, about 2 hours total time.

7. Melt 2 tbsp. butter in a saute pan and cook mushrooms until liquid evaporates. Add to finished stew along with the chopped parsley. Check for seasoning and serve over wide noodles. Drink a North Fork Pinot Noir, Merlot, or Cabernet Franc. *Serves 8*

Chicken in a Cocotte Bonne Femme

Ingredients	Amounts
Chicken, cut into pieces	1 whole chicken
Butter	¼ lb.
Olive oil	1 tbsp.
Coarse salt/ground black pepper	1 tbsp. each
White boiling onions	1 lb.
Carrots, cut into 2" chunks	2 cups
Parsnips, cut into 2" chunks	1 cup
Leeks, white part, diced	1 cup
Flour	¼ cup
Chardonnay	1 cup
Chicken broth	1 cup
Heavy cream	1 cup
Thyme	3 sprigs
Bay leaf	1
Black pepper	1 tsp.
Small white new potatoes	12
White mushrooms, whole	12
Parsley, chopped	¼ cup

Procedure

1. Bring one quart of water to a boil and blanch the white boiling on-ions for 2 minutes. Remove and peel with a small knife and set aside.

2. Heat a heavy casserole or Dutch oven and add a tbsp. each of butter and olive oil. Season the chicken pieces with salt and pepper and brown them in batches, being careful not to crowd them.

3. Remove the chicken and brown the onions in the same fat. Remove onions and brown the carrots and parsnips, adding more butter if necessary. Add the leeks, cooking at low heat until soft. Add the flour to make a roux and cook until lightly browned.

4. Whisk in the Chardonnay and bring to a boil. Gradually add the chicken broth and return to boil. Simmer for 5 minutes and add heavy cream. Add back the chicken and vegetables along with the bay leaf, black pepper, and thyme. Bring to a boil on the stove, cover, and place in a 300 degree oven. Cook in the oven for 1 hour and check to see if chicken is done. Meanwhile, boil the new potatoes and saute the mushrooms in 1 tbsp. of butter and add to the casserole with the chopped parsley. Serve with a barrel-fermented Chardonnay. *Serves 4*

Lobster Risotto

Ingredients	Amounts
Lobster, live, 1¼ lb.	2
Water	2 qts.
Chardonnay	1 cup
Pickling spice	1 tbsp.
Coriander seeds	1 tbsp.
Fennel seeds	1 tbsp.
Bay leaves	3
Thyme, dried	1 tsp.
Coarse salt	1 tbsp.
Black peppercorns, crushed	12
Lemons, cut in half	2
Olive oil	2 tbsp.
Shallots, chopped	¼ cup
Carrots, diced	¼ cup
Fresh fennel bulb, diced	¼ cup
Arborio rice	1½ cups
Butter, unsalted	2 tbsp.
Fresh tarragon, chopped	2 tbsp.
Fresh peas or zucchini, diced	2 cups

Procedure

1. In a big soup pot, combine the water, pickling spice, coriander, fennel, bay leaves, thyme, salt and pepper. Squeeze the lemon halves into the broth and add the lemons. Simmer this court bouillon for 30 minutes before adding the live lobsters. Cover and bring to a boil. Reduce heat and simmer for 15 minutes. Remove lobsters, cool, and remove meat. Cut meat into bite-sized pieces and strain the broth.

2. In a clean saucepan, heat the olive oil and add the shallots, carrots, and fennel. Saute for 3 minutes and add the rice. Stir the rice until coated with oil, and add the wine. Cook until wine is absorbed and add the broth a cup at a time, stirring to incorporate.

3. When the rice is tender and creamy, stir in the butter, the tarragon, and the peas. Fold in the lobster meat and serve with a barrel-fermented Chardonnay. *Serves 4*

Striped Bass Schnitzel
with Wine-Infused Sauerkraut

Ingredients	Amounts
Striped bass fillet, bones and skin removed	2 lb.
Sauerkraut, refrigerated	2 lbs.
Lemon Juice	1 tbsp.
Dry Riesling wine	2 cups
Coarse salt and pepper	1 tsp. each
Flour	1 cup
Egg, beaten	1
Milk	1 cup
Panko (Japanese breadcrumbs)	2 cups
Butter, unsalted	2 tbsp.
Olive oil	2 tbsp.
Bacon	4 strips
Green seedless grapes, cut in half	2 cups
Coarse salt and pepper to taste	

Procedure

1. Cut the bass fillet along the lateral line into two long pieces. Remove any small bones along this line. Cut the pieces into ¼" thick cutlets about 4" long. You should have 8 pieces. Sprinkle them with lemon juice and salt and pepper.

2. Set up a breading station by placing the flour in one pie tin and the Panko in another. Combine the beaten egg and milk in a bowl. Dredge the fish in the flour, then in the milk, and finally in the Panko. At service time heat the butter and oil in a large saute pan and cook fish until golden, about 3 minutes per side. It should flake easily with a fork.

3. Drain the sauerkraut in a colander and rinse under cold water. Squeeze completely dry.

4. Brown the bacon in a saute pan and remove. Chop the bacon and set aside. Add the sauerkraut to the bacon drippings and cook 5 minutes at low heat. Add the Riesling and simmer for about 20 minutes, uncovered, until wine is absorbed into sauerkraut. Stir in the grapes and the reserved bacon. Check for seasoning. (continued...)

5. Place the sauerkraut on the plates and the fish portions on top. Accompany this dish with potato dumplings, spaetzle, or mashed potatoes. Drink a dry (trocken) Riesling. *Serves 4*

Thai Curried Mussel Soup

Ingredients	Amounts
Mussels, rinsed & cleaned	3 lb
Onions, chopped	1 cup
Olive oil	1 tbsp.
Garlic, minced	1 tbsp
Ginger, minced	1 tbsp
White wine	1 cup
Lemon zest	from 1 lemon
Lemon juice	from 1 lemon
Orange juice	from 1 orange
Chicken broth	1½ cups
Coconut milk	1½ cups
Curry powder	1 tbsp
Thai chili paste	1 tsp
Soy sauce	1 tbsp
Cilantro, chopped	2 tbsp
Scallion, minced	2 tbsp

Procedure

1. Heat the oil in a large soup pot and add the onions, garlic, and ginger. Saute for 2 minutes and add the wine and lemon zest. Bring to a boil and simmer until reduced by one half.

2. Add the chicken broth, coconut milk, curry powder, chili paste, soy sauce, lemon and orange. Simmer for 20 minutes.

3. Add the mussels and bring back to the boil. Cook, covered, until mussels open and are fully cooked, about 5 minutes. Remove the mussels from the broth with a slotted spoon and cool.

4. Remove mussel meat and discard the shells. Add mussels back to the broth and check for seasoning. Serve in shallow bowls and garnish with the chopped cilantro and scallion. Drink a Gewurztraminer or Riesling from the North Fork, Germany, or Alsace. *Serves 4 to 6*

Sauteed Bay Scallops and Riesling

Ingredients	Amounts
Bay scallops, Peconic Bay if possible	1 lb.
Riesling, dry	1 cup
Flour	1 cup
Coarse salt and pepper	½ tsp. each
Olive oil	2 tbsp.
Butter, unsalted	2 tbsp.
Shallots, chopped	½ cup
Garlic, minced	1 tsp.
Tarragon, chopped	1 tbsp.
Italian parsley, chopped	1 tbsp.
Arugula, stemmed and rinsed	4 cups

Procedure

1. Place the flour in a bowl and season with the salt and pepper. Toss the scallops in this mixture and shake excess flour off with a sifter.

2. Heat the oil and butter in a large saute pan until sizzling. Add the scallops in batches, being careful not to overcrowd them. Remove quickly when golden brown and set aside.

3. To the drippings add the shallots and garlic and reduce the heat. Add the Riesling, scraping up the brown bits in the pan. Reduce the wine by half and add back the scallops. Stir in the tarragon and parsley and check for seasoning.

4. In a separate saucepan, add the rinsed arugula, cover, and heat very briefly until wilted. Place the arugula on 4 small plates and serve the scallops over it as a first course. Drink a dry Riesling from the North Fork or Germany. *Serves 4 as first course or 2 as an entree*

Wine as a Cooking Medium

When wine is used as the poaching liquid or is used to steam the dish, then it becomes the cooking medium, much like water or stock. Usually the lighter bodied, stainless steel fermented wines are used because poaching and steaming are methods used for more delicate foods and lighter sauces. The flavor of the primary food is preserved and accentuated with fresh herbs.

Mussels Marniere

Ingredients	Amounts
Mussels, soaked and rinsed	3 lbs.
Butter	2 tbsp.
Garlic, minced	1 tbsp.
Shallots, chopped	½ cup
Leeks, white part, diced	½ cup
Bay leaves	2
Sea salt and black pepper	1 tsp. each
Sauvignon blanc	1 cup
Heavy cream	1 cup
Chopped parsley	¼ cup

Procedure

1. In a large soup pot, melt the butter and add the garlic, shallots, leeks, and bay leaves. Saute until soft and add the mussels, salt and pepper, and wine. Cover, bring to a boil, and cook until all mussels open fully, about 10 minutes.

2. Remove the mussels with a slotted spoon and let cool. Discard top shells and place the mussels in shallow soup bowls for service.

3. Strain the cooking liquid into a saucepan and reduce by half. Remove from the heat and stir in the heavy cream and chopped parsley. Check for seasoning and pour over mussels. Serve with Sauvignon Blanc wine from the North Fork. *Serves 6*

Poached Salmon with White Wine Sauce

Ingredients	Amounts
6-oz. pieces of salmon fillet	6
Chardonnay	1 cup
Water	1 cup
Red onion, sliced	1 cup
Celery, diced	½ cup
Carrots, diced	½ cup
Peppercorns	6
Bay leaf	1
Thyme	3 sprigs
Parsley stems	6
Butter	2 tbsp.
Flour	3 tbsp.
Milk	2 cups
Coarse salt and pepper	1 tsp. each
Nutmeg	¼ tsp.
Lemon juice and zest	1 lemon
Fresh dill, chopped	1 tbsp.

Procedure

1. Make a court bouillon, or poaching liquid, by combining the wine, water, onions, celery, carrots, peppercorns, bay leaf, thyme, and parsley stems in a saucepan. Bring to a boil, simmer for 20 minutes and strain.

2. Spray a shallow saute pan with no-stick. Place the salmon in the pan, sprinkle with coarse salt and pepper, and pour the court bouillon over them to cover. Bring to a boil and simmer until fish is just cooked, about 5 minutes. Remove salmon to a warm plate and set aside.

3. Strain poaching liquid into a saucepan and reduce by half. In a separate pan, melt the butter and stir in the flour to make a roux. Cook briefly and whisk in the milk and seasonings. Add the reduced poaching liquid and cook until lightly thickened. Finish with the lemon juice, zest, and chopped dill. Serve sauce over salmon with boiled potatoes and a crisp Chardonnay. *Serves 6*

Wine in a Sauce

Much of our cooking involves grilling, pan-searing, and oven-roasting protein foods that are better when served with a sauce. The sauce heightens the flavors, adds richness, and gives the food a moist, tender texture and mouth feel. Wine is very effective when it becomes the principle or secondary ingredient in a sauce, whether it is a last-minute pan sauce, or a complex classical preparation.

Sauteed Pork Cutlets with Gewurztraminer

Ingredients	Amounts
Pork Cutlets, 4 oz., pounded thin	8
Gewurztraminer	½ cup
Coarse salt and pepper	1 tsp. each
Flour	½ cup
Butter and Olive Oil	1 tbsp. each
Shallots, chopped	½ cup
Thyme	1 tsp.
Ground Cumin	1 tsp.
Flour	1 tbsp.
Chicken broth	½ cup
Cilantro, chopped	¼ cup

Procedure

1. Season the pork cutlets with the coarse salt and pepper and dust lightly in flour. Heat the butter and olive oil in a large saute pan and brown the cutlets in batches at medium high heat until golden on both sides. Remove cutlets and set aside.

2. To the drippings add the shallots, thyme, and cumin. Cook briefly, stir in the flour and cook until lightly browned.

3. Whisk in the wine and chicken broth and bring to a boil. Add back the pork cutlets and simmer about 10 minutes.

4. Garnish with the cilantro and serve with Gewurztraminer.
   Serves 4

Sauces for Steak

Brown sauce

This sauce requires making a natural stock that becomes a brown sauce. The reduced wine is then added to finish. It takes a little extra effort to make all this from scratch, but there is no real substitute, and the final result will transform a filet mignon into a masterpiece of culinary art.

Ingredients	Amounts
Veal bones (knuckles, marrow bones)	3 lbs.
Onion, peeled and quartered	1
Carrots, chopped	3
Celery stalks, chopped	2
Peppercorns, crushed	6
Thyme, dried	1 tsp.
Bay leaves	2
Garlic	4 cloves
Sea salt	1 tsp.
Flour	½ cup
Water	1½ quarts
Tomato puree	¾ cup
Leeks, chopped	½ cup

Procedure

1. Place the veal bones, onion, carrots, and celery in a roasting pan. Season with peppercorns, thyme, bay leaves, and sea salt. Roast in a 425 degree oven for 45 minutes.

2. Remove from oven, sprinkle bones with flour, and roast 15 minutes longer.

3. Transfer ingredients to stock pot and deglaze roasting pan with a cup of water, scraping all drippings from the pan. Add this to the stock pot along with the water, tomato puree and the leeks. Simmer for three hours, skimming any scum that comes to the surface. Cool overnight, or skim as much fat as possible from the surface and continue recipe. *Makes about 1 quart*

Bordelaise sauce

Ingredients	Amounts
Brown sauce (from above)	1 quart
Butter	1 tbsp.
Shallots, chopped	½ cup
Merlot or Cabernet Sauvignon	2 cups
Lemon juice	1 tbsp.
Parsley, chopped	2 tbsp.
Butter, cold, cut in pieces	2 tbsp.

Procedure

1. Melt butter in a saucepan and add shallots. Cook until soft and add red wine. Simmer until reduced by half.

2. Add brown sauce (with surface fat removed) to reduced wine and simmer 30 minutes. Finish with lemon juice and parsley, Check for seasoning and swirl in cold butter just before serving. Serve with grilled steaks accompanied with a full-bodied Long Island wine. *Makes about 1 quart*

Sauteed Halibut, Beurre Blanc

Ingredients	Amounts
Halibut fillet, boneless, skinless, cut into ¼"-thick slices	1½ lbs.
Coarse salt and black pepper	1 tsp. each
Flour	½ cup
Unsalted butter	4 tbsp.
Sauvignon Blanc	½ cup
Lemon juice	2 tbsp.
Shallots, minced	½ cup
Cold, unsalted butter, cut up	8 oz. (2 sticks)
Chopped Italian parsley	¼ cup

Procedure

1. Season the halibut slices with salt and pepper and dust lightly in the flour.

2. Heat a large saute pan and add 2 tbsp. of the butter. Saute the halibut in batches, cooking until opaque and just cooked. Remove and keep warm.

3. Add the wine to the pan along with the lemon juice and shallots. Cook at high heat until reduced to about 2 tbsp. of liquid.

4. Whisk in the cold butter on low heat until smooth and creamy. Strain if desired and add the parsley. Check for seasoning and serve with Sauvignon Blanc wine. *Serves 4*

Using Wine as a Marinade

A marinade is a great way to add flavor and help tenderize less tender cuts of meat. When wine is used instead of vinegar or lemon juice, it provides the acidity, but also converts to a flavorful sauce at service time. The following example uses Port, a fortified wine, that is highly flavored and goes well with citrus fruit.

Marinated Skirt Steak (or Flank Steak)

Ingredients	Amounts
Skirt steak	3 lbs.
Port wine	2 cups
Olive oil	2 tbsp.
Orange juice and zest	from 1 orange
Red onion, sliced	2 cups
Thyme, fresh	2 tbsp.
Cinnamon stick	1
Cloves, whole	3
Cornstarch	1 tbsp.
Water, cold	1 tbsp.

Procedure

1. Combine the port, olive oil, orange juice and zest, thyme, onion, cinnamon, and cloves. Place in a bowl (or zip-lock bag) and marinate for 2 hours.

2. Remove steak and cook on chargrill. Strain marinade into saucepan and bring to a boil. Dissolve cornstarch in water and whisk into sauce. Serve with a Cabernet Franc or Syrah from Long Island. *Serves 4*

Marinated Sirloin Steak

Ingredients	Amounts
Top butt sirloin steak	3 lbs.
Olive oil	2 tbsp.
Red wine	½ cup
Balsamic vinegar	1 tbsp.
Soy sauce	1 tbsp.
Garlic, minced	1 tbsp.
Bay leaves, crumbled	2
Fresh thyme	3 sprigs
Cracked black pepper	1 tsp.
Coarse salt	1 tsp.

Procedure

1. Combine all ingredients except the steak in a bowl.

2. Cut the steak into 4 portions and place in a zip lock bag. Pour the marinade into the bag and refrigerate 4 hours or more.

3. Dry the steak off with paper towels and warm to room temperature. Cook over charcoal to desired doneness.

4. Strain marinade into a small saucepan and reduce to a glaze. Drizzle over steak at service time. Serve with a Cabernet Sauvignon or other full-bodied red wine. *Serves 4*

MATCHING FOOD AND WINE

"Man has been accorded by a kindly nature four stout companions to sustain and console him on his terrestial pilgrimage. They are wine, spirits, fortified wine, and beer. These drinks provide solace, relaxation, and stimulus that a man needs if he is to complete with eqanimity his arduous and often arid journey.

"The highball, the cocktail, and the glass of beer have helped so many of us to unwind, to make the transition from one kind of moment to another, totally different one. Wine, on the other hand, fills a somewhat different aspect of our need. Wine is more subtle and is best when accompanied by food."
— Alec Waugh, *"Wines and Spirits"* 1968

Wine enormously enhances the pleasure of the table. And wine that has been selected specifically to complement a particular dish increases the enjoyment value of both the food and the wine.

A meal accompanied by wine is taken slowly. First, the appearance of the food makes an impact with its colors and arrangement on the plate. Then the appearance of the wine, whether ruby red or straw yellow, resting in a beautiful crystal glass, also draws attention. Often the wine signals the official beginning of the meal with a customary toast. This is also the beginning of warm conversation between the participants. Next come the aromas of food and wine which excite the palate and ideally complement rather than clash with each other. All of this has happened before a single bite of food has been consumed. Some people feel that many of these rituals are a waste of precious time, but the reality is that slow consumption of food, wine, and conversation is one of the healthiest things that you can do.

Having wine that matches the food being served is only important in that it contributes to the overall enjoyment of the meal, just as the other elements do. And, like the elements of dining, it is very subjective, surrounded by culture, tradition, and personal preferences.

Physiology also plays a role. The basic tastes that we perceive are sweet, sour, bitter, salt, and perhaps umami (the taste created by glutamate). Food embodies all of these, while wine only includes the first three. The combination of these tastes in a particular dish, along with their intensity, influences the choice of wine. The way the food and wine feel in the mouth describes the weight and texture. A food can be delicate or robust, light or heavy. A wine can be lean with bracing acidity or it can be full bodied with loads of fruit.

Matching the weight of food and wine is more important than matching flavors. Thus, we enjoy a "big wine" that 'stands up" to rich food. Or we like a "crisp, light wine" that doesn't overpower our food. We also find that a wine with some residual sugar or an aromatic fruit component is able to complement spicy foods better than a bone dry wine. In situations where we are having more than one wine with our meal, the progression of wine is much like the progression of food: light before heavy; young before old; dry before sweet; and simple before complex.

As far as food is concerned, the cooking method and accompanying sauces and garnishes are more important than the food itself. If you delicately poach a fillet of salmon in white wine and serve it with steamed vegetables with dill and lemon, you will want to serve a crisp Chardonnay, Riesling, or Sauvignon Blanc. But if you place the salmon fillet on a cedar plank and roast it on a grill with duchess potatoes and serve it with hollandaise sauce, you are going to want to drink a toasty, barrel-fermented Chardonnay. The leaner the food, the leaner the wine. With rich food and sauces you want rich wines.

The geographical and cultural matching of food and wine is also important, but in a more intangible way. In a market where a particular wine is available anywhere in the world, does it matter where the wine comes from? Is there any advantage to drinking local wine with local food? And does the cultural background of the food require a similar cultural background in the wine? Variety is the spice of life, and we are very fortunate to live in a region where so much food and wine are available from around the world. It would seem pretty dumb to not take advantage of this great opportunity. When so much is available, price and marketing often determine our choices. But there is a synergy that comes from eating local food that is accompanied by local wine, and the style of Long Island wines is very food-friendly. Perhaps it is because each bottle comes with a story and each dish comes with ingredients from a farm that we can identify. Perhaps we know some of the people involved in production. Somehow they just taste better together.

The cultural side of food and wine is also interesting. We make a pasta dish with shrimp, olive oil, garlic, basil, and sun dried tomato and it seems to taste better with a Pinot Grigio, regardless of the wine's origin or quality. What we eventually find out is that the world of food and wine is infinite, controversial, and always exciting. The emotional, intangible side of what we eat and drink and why is one of life's great mysteries.

Wine and Cheese

The heightened interest in high-quality estate bottled wine has been accompanied by an equally heightened interest in cheese. Cheese shops and farmer's markets have proliferated, along with a wider and better selection at supermarkets. On the North Fork, Catapano has led the way as a producer of goat cheese, garnering national attention for its quality.

Wine, cheese and bread are natural companions, as they all involve yeast, and wine and cheese require aging, which results in complex flavors. Having wine and cheese together with bread, crackers and fresh fruit has been an age-old tradition for centuries. But does it matter which wine you drink with a specific cheese?

The answer is yes. The flavors of the cheese will enhance the flavors of the wine if matched properly. Here are a few guidelines:

- *Drink crisp white wine and sparkling wine with soft, creamy cheese; Chardonnay with brie, camembert, gouda and fontina.*

- *Blue cheese is especially compatible with good quality dessert wines. Roquefort with Sauternes and Stilton with Port are classic matches. Gorgonzola, Maytag and Danish blue go well with our local late-harvest wines and our local Port.*

- *The popular goat and sheep milk cheeses that have a tangy flavor are very good with young, aromatic Sauvignon Blanc, Pinot Grigio and dry Riesling.*

- *Hard, aged cheeses such as cheddar, emmentaler, parmigiano-reggiano and aged asiago are best with full-bodied red wine. Their deep, natural flavors compliment a quality red wine's complexities.*

Stainless Steel Chardonnay

When the Chardonnay grape is picked ripe, destemmed, and gently pressed into juice (or must) and then placed in a sealed stainless steel tank to ferment, it will result in a clean, crisp wine that has simple fruit aromas and lively acidity. Chardonnay of this style has become increasingly popular because it is very food-friendly and usually low in cost. The clean, refreshing, mouth-clensing taste is reminiscent of lemons and green apples. The medium weight and the neutral flavor of stainless Chardonnay make it the perfect wine for flavorful foods that are simply cooked. By itself it may be a little tart, but with sauteed chicken breasts or shrimp scampi it becomes the perfect match. The quality of the wine comes from the care of the grapes in the vineyard — not the machinations of the winemaker in the cellar.

Chicken Piccata

Ingredients	Amounts
Chicken cutlets, ¼" thick	2 lbs.
Coarse salt/black pepper	1 tsp. each
Flour	1 cup
Olive oil	2 tbsp.
Butter	1 tbsp.
Shallots, chopped	2 tbsp.
Garlic, minced	1 tbsp.
Flour	1 tbsp.
Chicken broth	1 cup
Chardonnay	½ cup
Lemon zest + thin lemon slices	from ½ lemon
Lemon juice	from ½ lemon
Ground pepper	½ tsp.
Chopped parsley	2 tbsp.

Procedure

1. Sprinkle chicken cutlets with the salt and pepper and dredge in flour. Heat the oil and butter in a large saute pan and cook cutlets at high heat until golden on each side, about 5 minutes. Cook in batches so as to not crowd the pan. Remove chicken and keep warm.

2. Add the shallots and garlic and cook until soft. Add the flour and cook another 3 minutes. Whisk in the chicken broth and Chardonnay and bring to a boil.

3. Add back the cooked chicken along with any juices. Add the lemon slices, zest, and juice and simmer for 5 minutes. Season with the pepper and garnish with parsley. Serve over linguine with a crisp Chardonnay. *Serves 4*

Shrimp Scampi

Ingredients	Amounts
Jumbo shrimp, shells on (16–20)	2 lbs.
Coarse salt and black pepper	1 tsp. each
Cornstarch	2 tbsp.
Olive oil	2 tbsp.
Unsalted butter	1 tbsp.
Garlic, minced	2 tbsp.
Chardonnay	¼ cup
Lemon zest + thin lemon slices	from ½ lemon
Lemon juice	from ½ lemon
Chopped parsley	2 tbsp.
Red pepper flakes	¼ tsp.

Procedure

1. Peel and devein shrimp, removing tails. Cut deeply along the top to butterfly and flatten them on a cutting board. Sprinkle the salt and pepper over them and, using a sieve, dust them with the cornstarch.

2. Heat the oil in a large saute pan and cook the shrimp at high heat. Do them in batches so as to not crowd the pan. Do not overcook. Remove the shrimp and add the butter and garlic to the drippings. Cook briefly and add the Chardonnay.

3. Add back the shrimp, lemon zest and slices, and lemon juice. Simmer 3 minutes and garnish with parsley and red pepper flakes. Check for seasoning, and serve over rice with stainless steel Chardonnay from the North Fork. *Serves 4*

Yuca-Crusted Flounder with Corn Sauce

Ingredients	Amounts
Corn, fresh, cut off the cob	4 ears
Butter, unsalted	4 tbsp.
Fresh thyme	2 sprigs
Coarse salt and pepper	½ tsp. each
Garlic, minced	1 tsp.
Lemon juice	2 tbsp.
Lemon zest	from 1 lemon
Chopped parsley	1 tbsp.
Flounder fillets	4 (about 2 lbs.)
Yuca, peeled, ends cut off	1 yuca
Olive oil	2 tbsp.

Procedure

1. Melt the butter in a saucepan and add the thyme. Cook until butter begins to brown and add the corn kernels. Season with salt and pepper and cook, covered, at low heat for 5 minutes.

2. Remove half the corn with a slotted spoon and place it in a food processor along with the garlic and lemon juice. Puree until smooth and add it back to the corn in the pan. Add the lemon zest and chopped parsley.

3. Cut the peeled yuca in half lengthwise and then in quarters. Slice off the small, purplish core and place in cold water to prevent browning. Shred the yuca with a box grater and set aside.

4. Lay the flounder fillets on a piece of waxed paper, Season with salt and pepper and press the shredded yuca into both sides of the fish fillets with your fingers.

5. Heat a saute pan and add the olive oil. Cook the flounder until golden, about 3 minutes per side. Do not crowd the pan. Serve over the warm corn sauce and garnish with chopped parsley and lemons. Serve over braised greens with a stainless steel North Fork Chardonnay. *Serves 4*

Barrel-Fermented Chardonnay

Chardonnay is the white wine grape grown around the world. Classically, it is the grape of French white Burgundies such as Meursault, Puligny Montrachet, and Pouilly Fuisse. It is also the grape used in Chablis and one of the grapes used in Champagne. Chardonnay is often called the "winemakers grape" because it can be made in so many styles. The two most popular are stainless steel Chardonnay and barrel-fermented Chardonnay. They result in very different flavors and aromas and are both good accompaniments to food — but not the same food.

Barrel-Fermented Chardonnay is bigger, oakier, and richer than its simpler stainless steel cousin. When the yeast reacts with the sugars in the grape juice, fermentation results. Fermentation produces carbon dioxide and alcohol, but also creates heat. When fermentation occurs within a barrel it extracts tannins and vanilla flavors from the wood. Vintners use oak from famous locations in France such as Limousin, Nevers, and Troncais. They also use American oak and barrels from other countries as well. When new, it imparts a very pronounced flavor to the wine and when used it imparts a subtler flavor.

After the initial fermentation the wine is "racked" off the oak barrels into different ones to continue the aging process. At this time it often undergoes a malolactic fermentation which is either natural or induced. The malic acid is converted to lactic acid, resulting in a smoother texture with reduced acidity and more complex flavors. The green apple aroma is replaced with a toasty, buttery, more cheese-like aroma. If the wine remains balanced with strong fruit character and good acidity to offset the new flavors it will turn out delicious and the perfect accompaniment to rich, buttery, cheesy, foods.

Fettuccine Alfredo

This recipe is the perfect accompaniment to a barrel-fermented Chardonnay. The robust texture of handmade fettuccine is worth the extra trouble and gives the dish the "weight" it needs to accompany a big Chardonnay. If desired, saute some bay scallops or steam a lobster to toss with the fettuccine — or enjoy it as it is.

Ingredients	Amounts
Flour	2 cups
Large eggs	4
Unsalted butter	4 tbsp.
Heavy cream	1½ cup
Grated parmesan (good quality)	1½ cup
Coarse salt and pepper	1 tsp. each

Procedure

1. Pour the flour onto a work surface, shape it into a mound, and scoop out a hollow in the center. Break the eggs into the hollow and beat them with a fork for a minute. Using the fork, draw flour over the eggs and stir until eggs are no longer runny.

2. Use your hands to work the flour into the eggs until you have a moist dough. Then wash your hands, scrape the area clean, and dust it with flour.

3. Knead the dough with the heel of your hand by flattening it, folding it in half, and flattening it again. Do this for 10 minutes until the dough becomes smooth and elastic.

4. Cut the dough into 12 pieces, flatten them, and put them on a towel. Set up a pasta machine (or roll them out by hand with a rolling pin). Roll each piece through the machine at the widest setting, then roll again at successively narrower settings until you reach the #3 setting. Each dough should be about 12" × 3" wide. Let these strips rest on the towels about 15 minutes, uncovered, to dry before cutting them.

5. Run pieces of dough through the fettuccine cutter and wrap the fettuccine around your hand to make a nest. Place the nests back on the towel. Do not cover or refrigerate. You can leave it to dry for 24 hours or more if desired.
   (continued...)

6. Boil the fresh pasta in at least 4 quarts of water until tender. Drain and place back in the pot on the stove. Add the butter, cream, grated cheese, and seasoning. Place on low heat and stir until smooth and hot. Serve with barrel-fermented Chardonnay. *Serves 4*

Pan-Seared Sea Scallops with Potato Gnocchi

Ingredients	Amounts
Fresh Sea Scallops, cut in half horizontally	1 lb.
Yukon gold potatoes in their skins	½ lb.
Parmesan cheese, grated	2 tbsp.
Coarse salt	1 tsp.
Nutmeg, ground	¼ tsp.
Egg, beaten	1
Flour, all purpose	1 cup
Water, boiling	4 quarts
Butter, unsalted	4 tbsp.
Chardonnay	¼ cup
Zest and juice from one lemon	1
Heavy cream	1 cup
Coarse salt and pepper	½ tsp. each
Italian parsley, chopped	¼ cup

Procedure

1. Boil the potatoes in 2 quarts of water until tender. When cool enough to handle, peel off the skins and force them through a potato ricer. Place potatoes in a bowl with the cheese, salt, nutmeg, beaten egg and flour. Mix together with a wooden spoon and turn out onto a floured surface and knead gently into a dough, adding a little flour if needed.

2. Let the dough rest for 10 minutes and cut into 6 equal pieces. With your hands, roll each piece on a floured surface into a rope about 1" thick. Cut the rope into 1" pieces.

3. Hold a dinner fork in one hand and roll each gnocchi over the tines of the fork, pressing a small hole in the center as you roll. You will create grooves on one side and a hole on the other. (continued...)

4. Bring 4 quarts of water to a boil and cook the gnocchi, stirring gently, until they float, about 5 minutes. Remove them with a slotted spoon to a sheet pan. Set aside.

5. Heat a large saute pan and add 2 tbsp. of the butter, When it foams, saute the scallops in batches, being careful not to burn the bottom of the pan. Remove the scallops as they turn golden and place them on the sheet pan. Melt the remaining butter in the same pan and saute the gnocchi until they are lightly browned. Remove them and set aside.

6. Deglaze the pan with the lemon juice and the Chardonnay. Scrape the brown bits from the bottom of the pan and add the heavy cream and lemon zest. Add back the gnocchi and scallops and season to taste with the salt and pepper. Garnish with the parsley and serve with Long Island barrel-fermented Chardonnay. *Serves 4*

Sauvignon Blanc

A dry white wine that is in high demand as people tire of the ubiquitous Chardonnay. Unlike Chardonnay, Sauvignon Blanc always has a distinctive aroma and a flinty texture. It has a straw color and a grassy smell and is often described as "herbal". At its best, the taste can be wonderfully refreshing with its piercing acidity. At its worst it can smell like cat urine and have a vegetal taste like left-over vegetable cooking water. The Loire Valley in France is famous for its Sancerre and Pouilly Fumé, both made from Sauvignon Blanc. New Zealand is the most famous new world growing area for the grape. The North Fork continues to plant more Sauvignon Blanc in an effort to keep up with demand. Some Sauvignon Blanc is being barrel-fermented, but most is fermented and aged in stainless steel. Sauvignon Blanc is the perfect accompaniment to raw oysters and is the perfect wine from which to make Beurre Blanc sauce. It is also a great match for a soft, artisanal goat cheese, such as made by Catapano on the North Fork.

Oysters on the Half Shell, Mignonette

Ingredients	Amounts
Oysters, fresh in the shell, farmed or wild	2 dozen
Red wine vinegar	½ cup
Cider vinegar	2 tbsp
Lemon juice	2 tsp
Shallots, minced	2 tbsp
Black pepper, freshly ground	2 tbsp

1. For the sauce Mignonette, mix the vinegars and lemon juice together in a small glass bowl. Then add the shallots and the pepper.

2. Rinse the oysters in cold running water. If they are muddy, scrub them with a vegetable brush. Set them on a sheet pan.

3. To shuck wild oysters, place them bottom side down on a towel, on a solid table. Using an oyster glove or a towel, grasp the oyster with your left hand (if right-handed) and hold the oyster firmly against the table. Insert a straight-bladed stiff oyster knife into the hinge and press down into the "sweet spot" where the shells meet. Wiggle the point until the knife slips through the opening, then twist firmly to pop the top shell loose. Run the knife along the top until you cut through the adductor muscle. The shell will now pop off easily. When shucking farmed oysters, it is better to insert the knife in the side so as to avoid shattering the more delicate shell. Otherwise proceed as above.

4. If the above methods give you trouble, use pliers to snip off a small piece of the tip of the shell and insert a straight-bladed knife into the opening, before twisting the top loose. It may be necessary to rinse some oysters under cold water to get rid of any shell pieces that have broken off.

5. When open, place the oysters on crushed ice and serve with the sauce. The guests should sauce their oysters at the last minute before eating them. Drink a chilled Sauvignon Blanc wine from Long Island or around the world. *Serves 4*

Corn Cakes with Lump Crabmeat

Ingredients	Amounts
Maryland lump crabmeat, picked over for cartilage	1 lb.
Corn on the cob, very fresh	4 ears
Eggs, beaten	3
Flour	¼ cup
Scallion, minced	1 cup
Tarragon, chopped	1 tbsp
Tabasco	few drops
Coarse salt and pepper	¼ tsp each
Olive oil	2 tbsp

Procedure

1. Scrape the kernels off the corn and steam very quickly over boiling water. Do not overcook. Rinse under cold water and set aside.

2. Break up the crabmeat with your hands and combine with the cooked corn in a bowl. In a separate bowl, beat the eggs and fold in the flour. Add the scallion, tarragon, Tabasco, salt and pepper. Gently fold in the crabmeat so that it just holds together. Form the mixture into small patties (about 2oz. each) and dust in a little flour.

3. Heat the olive oil in a large saute pan and cook the crab cakes at medium heat until golden brown on both sides. Serve with lemon, parsley, and Sauvignon Blanc wine. *Makes 8 appetizer portions*

Penne with Shrimp and Goat Cheese

Ingredients	Amounts
Penne, whole grain	1 lb.
Goat cheese, with basil and herbs, crumbled	6 oz.
Extra virgin olive oil	2 tbsp.
Shrimp, 16-20 jumbo, in the shell	1½ lb.
Garlic, minced	1 tbsp.
Sun-dried tomatoes	8
Red pepper flakes	½ tsp.
Broccoli rabe, coarsely chopped	1 bunch

Procedure

1. Bring 3 quarts of water to a boil and cook penne al dente, about 10 minutes. Save 1 cup of the cooking water.

2. Heat the olive oil in a large saute pan and cook the shrimp at high heat until they turn pink. Remove shrimp and cool. Peel and devein shrimp and cut in half lengthwise.

3. In the shrimp drippings, saute the garlic and sun-dried tomato until soft, about 3 minutes. Add the cup of pasta-cooking water and the broccoli rabe. Cover and cook briefly until broccoli is just tender, but still bright green. Remove from heat and add the red pepper flakes and the peeled shrimp. Combine with the penne and return to the heat. When hot, check for seasoning and sprinkle with the goat cheese. Serve with Sauvignon Blanc. *Serves 4*

Pinot Grigio

Pinot Grigio is the Italian wine that uses the Pinot Gris grape that is widely grown in Alsace and Germany. It has become immensely popular in recent years for its light body, crisp, unoaked acidity, and fresh fruit flavors. Several wineries on Long Island are producing Pinot Grigio. It best suits foods that are light in texture with aromatic seasoning and perhaps an Italian personality.

Pan-Seared Striped Bass with Crispy Skin, Grape Tomatoes, and Kalamata Olives

Ingredients	Amounts
Striped bass fillets, boneless, skin on	2 lbs.
Olive oil	2 tbsp.
Coarse salt and pepper	1 tsp. each
Kalamata olives, pitted	1 cup
Grape tomatoes, cut in half	2 cups
Garlic, minced	1 tbsp.
Basil, chopped	½ cup
Olive oil	1 tbsp.

Procedure

1. Cut the bass fillets into four equal portions, leaving the skin on. Rub them with the oil and season with salt and pepper.

2. Place the olives, tomatoes, garlic, and basil in a bowl.

3. Heat a cast iron skillet to high and coat the bottom with olive oil. When shimmering add the bass fillets skin side down. Do not crowd the pan. Carefully turn the fish with a metal spatula to avoid tearing the skin. Turn down the heat to medium and cook until flesh flakes easily and turns an opaque color, about 5 minutes.

4. Remove the fish to serving plates and add the tomato mixture along with a little more olive oil. Cook another 3 minutes and pour over the fish. Serve this dish with creamy polenta and a Pinot Grigio from Long Island or Italy. *Serves 4*

Riesling

Riesling has been grown in the Rhine and Mosel valleys of Germany from at least the 15th century. Germany still produces two thirds of the world's Riesling, but it is now grown in many other countries as well, including the United States. A small amount is produced on the North Fork. Riesling is a versatile grape variety that is very compatible with food. It is light-bodied and not aged in oak. Riesling has a distinctive floral aroma that is reminiscent of peaches, apples, and pears. Dry, or "trocken", Riesling can have a stony minerality and lively acidity that brings out the best in lean fish, such as flounder and cod. Off-dry, or "halbtrocken" Riesling goes very well with spicy Asian foods.

Roasted Codfish

Ingredients	Amounts
Cod fillet, cut into 4 portions	2 lbs.
Grapefruit juice	½ cup
Shallots, chopped	¼ cup
Coriander, ground	1 tsp.
Coarse salt and black pepper	1 tsp. each
Pink grapefruit, sectioned	1
Green seedless grapes, halved	1 cup
Kale, ribs removed, cut in 2" pieces	2 bunches
Olive oil	2 tbsp.
Cold butter	4 tbsp.
Cilantro, chopped	¼ cup

Procedure

1. Put the cod fillets into a bowl with the grapefruit juice, shallots, coriander, and salt and pepper. Refrigerate for up to 2 hours.

2. Remove the cod from the marinade, dry with a towel, and brush with olive oil. Place fish on a sheet pan, season with salt and pepper, and roast at 425 degrees until flesh turns opaque and flakes easily (about 15 minutes).

3. Remove the fish from the oven and pour the marinade over it along with the grapefruit and grapes. Place it back in the oven for 5 minutes.

4. Steam the kale in a separate pan until bright green and just cooked. Place the kale in the center of the plate and put the cod on top. Spoon the fruit around the cod and strain the juices left in the pan into a small saucepan. Bring this to a boil and swirl in the cold butter.

5. Pour the sauce over the fish and garnish with the chopped cilantro. Serve with dry Riesling. ***Serves 4***

Spicy Asian Pork Cutlets

Ingredients	Amounts
Pork cutlets, ¼" thick	2 lbs.
Soy sauce	¼ cup
Honey	2 tbsp.
Rice wine (or dry sherry)	1 tbsp.
Ginger, minced	1 tsp.
Five-spice powder	¼ tsp.
Ground black pepper	½ tsp.
Vegetable oil	2 tbsp.
Shiitake mushrooms, sliced	2 cups
Green beans, fresh, cut in 1" pieces	2 cups
Orange juice	¼ cup
Soy sauce	1 tbsp.
Sesame oil	1 tsp.
Ginger, minced	1 tsp.
Sugar	1 tsp.
Ground black pepper	½ tsp.
Cornstarch/cold water	1 tsp. each

Procedure

1. Place the pork, soy sauce, honey, rice wine, ginger, five-spice powder, and pepper in a casserole dish and refrigerate for up to 4 hours.

2. Heat a large saute pan and add 1 tbsp. of the oil. Wipe off cutlets with paper towels and brown them at medium high heat on both sides. Cook in batches to avoid crowding. Remove cutlets to a sheet pan and put them in a 200 degree oven.

3. To the drippings add the shiitake mushrooms and cook about 5 minutes. Add to the sheet pan.

4. Place another tbsp. of oil in the pan and saute the green beans at high heat about 3 minutes. When lightly brown, add them to the sheet pan.

5. Turn the heat down and add the orange juice, soy sauce, sesame oil, ginger, sugar, and pepper. Dissolve the cornstarch in the water and add to the sauce. Check for seasoning and pour over the pork and vegetables. Serve with rice and an off-dry Riesling.
Serves 4

Gewurztraminer

The most perfumed and mispronounced wine in the world, Gewurztraminer, especially from Alsace or Germany, has an aroma of gingerbread, lychee, and grapefruit. It is an assertive, spicy white wine that sometimes seems sweet, but is usually bone dry. It needs to be enjoyed with bold flavors such as you find in the famous "choucroute garni" of Alsace or in bold Asian dishes with ginger, Thai chili, and garlic. Some very good versions of Gewurztraminer are made on the North Fork.

Choucroute Garni

Ingredients	Amounts
Sauerkraut, fresh	1 lb.
Salt pork, sliced into 2" pieces	8 oz.
Onion, diced	1 cup
Carrots, diced	1 cup
Garlic, minced	2 tbsp.
Apples, tart, cooking style, peeled and diced	2
Chicken broth	1 cup
Gewurztraminer	½ cup
Juniper berries, chopped	1 tbsp.
Coarse salt and pepper	1 tsp. each
Bay leaves	2
Kielbasa, uncooked, cut in 2" chunks	1 lb.
Red potatoes, sliced with skins on, ¼" thick	2 cups
Knockwurst, cut into 2" pieces	1 lb.
Smoked ham, thick slice, cut up into 2" pieces	1 lb.

Procedure

1. Rinse the sauerkraut and squeeze it dry. Brown the salt pork in a Dutch oven and remove.

2. Add the onion, carrots, and garlic to the pork fat and cook briefly.

3. Add the apples and the sauerkraut to the pot along with the chicken broth, Gewurztraminer, and juniper berries. Season with the salt and pepper and the bay leaves (substitute ¼ cup gin for juniper berries if desired).

4. Add back the browned salt pork and bring to a boil, cover, and place in a 300 degree oven for 1 hour. Remove from the oven and add the kielbasa and potatoes. Return, covered, to the oven and cook for another 45 minutes.

5. Remove the pot and add the knockwurst and smoked ham. Continue cooking for 15 minutes. Serve with grainy mustard and Gewurztraminer wine. *Serves 4*

Thai Curried Seafood Stew

Ingredients	Amounts
Shrimp, raw, peeled and deveined	½ lb.
Bay scallops	½ lb.
Mussels, cleaned and rinsed	1 lb.
Olive oil	2 tbsp.
Leeks, chopped, white part	1 cup
Garlic, minced	1 tbsp.
Ginger, minced	1 tsp.
Curry powder	1 tbsp.
Jalepeno pepper, minced	1 tsp.
Coconut milk, unsweetened	2 cups
Chicken broth	½ cup
Gewurztraminer	½ cup
White rice, uncooked	¼ cup
White wine	½ cup
Lime juice and zest	from one lime
Cilantro, chopped	¼ cup

Procedure

1. Heat the olive oil in a soup pot and add the leeks, garlic, ginger, curry powder, and jalepeno pepper. Saute briefly and add the coconut milk, chicken broth, Gewurztraminer, and rice. Bring to a boil and simmer, covered, until rice is just tender, about 15 minutes.

2. Add the raw shrimp and scallops, cover, and simmer until seafood is cooked, another 15 minutes.

3. Separately, place the mussels in a soup pot with the wine and bring to the boil. When the mussels are open and fully cooked, remove them with a slotted spoon and set aside. Strain the broth and let any sediment settle to the bottom.

4. Stir the mussel broth and lime juice and zest into the stew. Check for seasoning and spoon the stew into shallow bowls. Garnish each portion with mussels and sprinkle with cilantro. Serve with Gewurztraminer wine. *Serves 4*

Merlot

Merlot is the signature grape of the North Fork after our first 35 years of experimentation. Vintage after vintage, it does pretty well in the vineyard, but more importantly, Merlot has emerged from our cellars with a personality of its own. At their best, North Fork Merlots are fruit-driven and elegant with aromas of blackberry, cassis, plums, and a little leather. They come in a wide variety of styles and price ranges and are used in almost all of our red wine blends.

Merlot is the grape most widely planted in Bordeaux. It is blended with Cabernet Sauvignon in the Medoc to soften the tannins and it is the primary grape of Pomerol and St. Emilion. Chateau Petrus, one of the world's most expensive wines, is made almost entirely from Merlot.

Merlot complements a wide range of foods. It is often medium-bodied and should be paired with foods that are not highly spiced or heavily sauced. Roast lamb and almost any duck preparation are delicious with Merlot, as are many sauteed veal and pork preparations. Merlot is like Chardonnay in that it pairs with many different foods depending on its style. A lighter, simpler Merlot is excellent with grilled tuna and salmon, while a full-bodied Merlot is very good with steak.

Pan-Seared Tuna
with Roasted Portabella Mushrooms

Ingredients	Amounts
Tuna Steaks, thick cut, 6 oz.	4
Olive oil	2 tbsp.
Coarse salt and pepper	1 tsp. each
Portabella mushrooms, with stems	4
Dried Porcini mushrooms	½ cup
Water, warm	1 cup
Merlot	1 cup
Black peppercorns	8
Fresh thyme	3 sprigs
Bay leaves	2
Kale, stems removed	4 cups
Cornstarch/cold water	1 tbsp. each

Procedure

1. Season the tuna steaks with salt and pepper and set aside.

2. Remove stems from portabella mushrooms, trim off the ends and chop coarsely.

3. Soak the Porcini mushrooms in the warm water for 20 minutes. Remove mushrooms and strain liquid through cheesecloth.

5. Place liquid, porcini mushrooms, chopped portabella stems, merlot, and seasonings into a saucepan and simmer for 45 minutes. Strain and reduce by half.

6. Place Portabella caps on a lightly oiled sheet pan. Roast in a 400 degree oven for 20 minutes. Heat ¼ cup water in a saute pan and wilt the kale by cooking, covered, for 5 minutes. Remove and place in portabella mushrooms.

7. Pan-sear tuna in olive oil until rare, about 2 minutes per side. Place tuna on portabella caps on top of wilted kale. Deglaze pan with reduced wine/mushroom stock and thicken lightly with the cornstarch and water solution. *Serves 4*

Roast Lamb with White Bean Casserole

Ingredients	Amounts
Boneless leg of lamb	about 4 lbs.
Garlic, slivers	2 cloves
Rosemary, fresh	1 tbsp.
Lemon juice	2 tbsp.
Coarse salt and ground black pepper	1 tsp. each
Onion, coarsely chopped	1 cup
Carrot, chopped	½ cup
Celery, chopped	½ cup
Flour	2 tbsp.
Chicken broth	1 cup
Merlot	½ cup

Procedure

1. Cut small slits in the lamb and insert the slivers of garlic. Combine the rosemary and lemon juice and rub over the lamb. Sprinkle with the salt and pepper and place in a roasting pan.

2. Surround the meat with the chopped onion, carrot, and celery. Place in a 300 degree oven and roast until the internal temperature is 135 degrees. Remove and keep warm.

3. Add the flour to the roasting pan and cook on top of the stove for 3 minutes. Stir in the chicken broth and Merlot and bring to a boil. Strain into a saucepan and simmer 5 minutes. Skim any surface fat and check for seasoning.

Ingredients - white bean casserole	Amounts
Cannellini beans, drained and rinsed	4 15oz. cans
Diced tomatoes	1 15 oz. can
Olive oil	2 tbsp.
Onion, chopped	1 cup
Garlic, minced	1 tbsp.
Thyme leaves	1 tbsp.
Bay leaves	2
Lemon zest	from 1 lemon
Chicken broth	1 cup
Panko (Japanese bread crumbs)	½ cup
Coarse salt and pepper	½ tsp. each

Procedure

1. Heat the oil in a saute pan and add the onion, garlic, thyme, bay leaves, and lemon zest. Saute 3 minutes and add the chicken broth. Bring to a boil and add the cannellini beans and tomatoes.

2. Transfer mixture to a casserole and sprinkle with panko. Season with salt and pepper and place in the oven with the lamb. Cook about 1 hour, or until crumbs are brown and beans are bubbly. Serve with lamb and a North Fork Merlot. *Serves 8*

Merlot, Cabernet Franc, and Pinot Noir – The Special Case of the Long Island Duck

The duck and Long Island share a long history. The sandy soil, easy access to water for ponds, and a good market in New York City made the East End a natural for duck farming. (Some of these same conditions make it a natural for wine). Since 1873, with the introduction of the first Pekin ducks, our local duck has become world famous. And even though commercial production peaked in 1968, the remaining producers still ship about 2 million ducks a year. These high quality ducks have been an important part of our growth as a culinary destination.

Recipes prepared with Long Island Duck also have a special relationship with Long Island wine. The rich, all-dark meat of a duck with its crispy, flavorful skin requires a medium-bodied wine with lively acidity and contrasting fruit flavor. Long Island Merlot, Cabernet Franc, and Pinot Noir all fill the bill perfectly. Variations in sauces and garnishes, cooking methods, and the level of seasoning help to determine which variety works best — or just your own personal taste. I can think of no food and wine combination that is more compatible than Long Island duck and our local wine.

Honey Glazed Roast Duck

Ingredients	Amounts
Long Island duck, whole, 6 lb.	1
Coarse salt and pepper	1 tsp. each
Onion, peeled, cut in half	1
Whole cloves	2
Bay leaves	2
Honey	¼ cup

Procedure

1. Remove the giblets and neck from the cavity and rinse the duck under cold water. Cut off the tail, the flap of skin at the neck, and the wing tips. Reserve these for stock. Rub the cavity with salt and pepper and place the onion, stuck with the cloves and bay leaves, inside.

2. Push the legs up against the breast and tie them with string. Puncture the skin with a sharp cooks fork, and tie the wings against the body with string. Brush the duck with honey and sprinkle with coarse salt and pepper.

3. Preheat the oven to 475 degrees. Put the duck, on its side, on a rack in a roasting pan. Roast for 20 minutes and turn duck to its other side. Roast for another 20 minutes and reduce the heat to 400 degrees. Place the duck breast side up on the rack and cook for 1½ hours. The skin will turn a dark lacquered color. If it begins to brown too much, place a loose piece of foil over the duck. When cooked, the legs and wings will wiggle with little resistance.

4. Remove the duck from the oven and cool for 20 minutes. Split into halves and remove the backbone and the interior rib bones. Then split into quarters and reheat just before serving.

Bigarade Sauce for Roast Duck

Ingredients	Amounts
Duck stock (or chicken broth)	3 cups
Brown sugar	½ cup
Red wine vinegar	⅓ cup
Butter	2 tbsp.
Flour	3 tbsp.

Whole orange	1
Whole lemon	1
Port wine	½ cup
Cinnamon stick	1
Whole cloves	3
Peppercorns	6
Currant jelly	1 tbsp.

Procedure

1. In a small saute pan, heat the sugar until it melts and stir until it begins to carmelize. Do not burn. Stir in the vinegar and cook until reduced to a thin syrup (this is called a Gastrique).

2. Melt the butter in a saucepan and stir in the flour to make a roux. Cook briefly and add the duck stock or broth. Cut the orange and lemon into quarters and squeeze into the sauce, adding the whole skin and pulp at the end. Add the wine, spices, and Gastrique from above and simmer for 30 minutes.

3. Stir in the currant jelly and taste the sauce for seasoning. Strain into a bowl and serve. Garnish the duck with orange slices and dried cherries which have been soaked in Port. *Serves 4*

Duck Ragout in Red Wine

Ingredients	Amounts
Long Island duck legs	8
for the stock	
Onion, chopped	1 cup
Carrot, chopped	½ cup
Celery, chopped	½ cup
Peppercorns	6
Bay leaf	1
Thyme	2 sprigs
for the ragout	
Pearl onions, peeled	2 cups
Whole white mushrooms	2 cups
Carrots, peeled and diced	½ cup
Garlic, minced	1 tbsp.
Flour	½ cup
Red wine	2 cups
Duck stock (or chicken broth)	2 cups
Bay leaf	1
Thyme	2 sprigs
Pepper, ground	1 tsp.
Parsley, chopped	¼ cup

Procedure

1. Bone out the duck legs and cut into 2" pieces. (leave skin on, but trim off fat).

2. Make the stock by placing the bones in a pan with the onion, carrot, and celery. Roast in a 425 degree oven until brown, about 30 minutes. Transfer bones and vegetables to a soup pot and almost cover with cold water. Deglaze the pan on the stove with 1 cup of water and add to the pot. Add the seasonings and cook for 2 hours. Strain and skim fat from surface.

3. In a heavy casserole or Dutch oven brown the duck pieces at high heat, being careful not to burn the skin. Remove duck pieces with a slotted spoon and pour off most of duck fat. (reserve excess fat). Add the pearl onions to the pan and brown in the duck fat. Remove and brown the mushrooms in duck fat. Remove and set aside. (continued...)

4. Add the diced carrots and minced garlic to the pan and saute until soft. Add the flour to the pan to make a roux. (if necessary, add a little more duck fat). Add the wine and stock (or broth) and cook until lightly thickened.

5. Add back the duck pieces, the onions, and the mushrooms. Season with the bay leaf, thyme, and pepper. Bring to a boil, cover, and place in a 300 degree oven to cook until tender, about 1 hour. Skim any fat and stir in the parsley. Check for seasoning and serve.
Makes 4 portions

Pan-Seared Duck Breast, Beurre Rouge

Ingredients	Amounts
Whole Duck breasts, skin on, split in half	2
Coarse salt and ground black pepper	1 tsp each
Shallots, minced	¼ cup
Merlot	½ cup
Cold unsalted butter, cut in pieces	4 oz. (1 stick)

Procedure

1. Trim excess fat from duck breasts but leave skin on. Score skin with a sharp knife and season with the salt and pepper.

2. Using a cast iron skillet, sear the breasts skin side down at high heat until golden brown. Reduce heat, turn, and cook until medium rare, about 5 minutes. Remove and keep warm.

3. Pour off excess fat and add shallots and Merlot. Reduce to ¼ cup and swirl in cold butter. Slice duck on the bias and strain sauce over them. Serve with wild rice and Merlot. If desired, garnish with dried cherries or dried cranberries that have been hydrated in a little hot water. *Serves 4*

Chargrilled Duck Breasts
with Roasted Plum Sauce

Ingredients	Amounts
Long Island duck breasts (whole)	2
Coarse salt and ground black pepper	½ tsp. each
Fresh plums	12
Maple syrup	1 tbsp.
Merlot	1 cup

for the sauce

Merlot	2 cups
Maple syrup	2 tbsp.
Honey	1 tbsp.
Shallots, chopped	¼ cup
Beef broth	½ cup
Beach plum jam (or currant jelly)	1 tbsp.

Procedure

1. Split the duck breasts in half to make 4 portions. Trim off all excess fat, leaving the skin on. Score the skin with a sharp knife into criss-cross patterns. Sprinkle with salt and pepper.

2. Heat the oven to 350 degrees. Cut the plums in half and remove pits. Place them cut side down in a shallow pan. Mix the Merlot and maple syrup together and pour over plums. Roast for 30 minutes.

3. Meanwhile, combine the Merlot, maple syrup, honey, and shallots into a saucepan and reduce by half. Remove the plums from the oven and puree in a food processor along with all juices. Add to the reduced wine mixture, along with the beef broth. Season to taste with salt and pepper. If very tart, stir in the plum jam or jelly.

4. Grill duck breasts skin side down until golden brown, about 3 minutes. Turn and cook until medium rare, about 5 minutes more. Slice on the bias and serve with the sauce. *Serves 4*

Duck Spring Rolls

Ingredients	Amounts
Long Island duck legs	6
Napa cabbage, shredded	2 cups
Radicchio (or red cabbage)	1 cup
Red pepper, julienned into	
thin slivers	1 cup
Scallion, chopped	½ cup
Cilantro, chopped	¼ cup
Ginger, minced	1 tbsp.
Sesame oil	2 tbsp.
Red pepper flakes	½ tsp.
Coarse salt and black pepper	½ tsp.each
Spring roll skins, 8"	12
Egg white	1
Vegetable oil	4 cups
Hoisin sauce	½ cup

Procedure

1. Roast the duck legs on a sheet pan at 400 degrees for one hour. Remove and cool. Peel off skin and remove the bones. Shred the meat into small pieces and set aside. (**note:** use duck confit if you have it)

2. Heat a saute pan and add the sesame oil. Quickly stir-fry the vegetables, cilantro, and ginger for 3 minutes. Add the duck meat and cook another 2 minutes. Transfer to a bowl and season with the red pepper flakes, salt and pepper.

3. Soak each spring roll skin in warm water for 30 seconds before filling. Cover cutting board with plastic wrap and lay out spring roll skin. Mix egg white with a few drops of water and brush onto the skin. Place ¼ cup of filling in the center and pull up the bottom over the filling. Fold in the sides and roll tightly. Transfer to a sheet pan lined with plastic film and repeat until all filling is used.

4. At service time, heat the vegetable oil to 350 degrees in a deep pan. Deep fry the spring rolls until golden, about 4 minutes. Remove and drain on paper towels. Cut in half on the bias and serve with hoisin sauce on the side (drink Gewurztraminer with this dish). *Serves 4*

Cabernet Sauvignon

Cabernet is the classic red wine grape, made famous by the First Growths of Bordeaux and more recently by the blockbuster Cabernets of Napa Valley. Because of its massive tannins, high alcohol, and rich fruit, Cabernet is the most ageworthy of wines. When it is good, the aromas of cedar, leather, and tar are accompanied by a bouquet of blackberry, currants, plums, and cassis. Here on the North Fork we make some delicious Cabernet, but not in the big California style. At their best, ours are more like the blends of Bordeaux, with more subtle flavors and an elegant style. Some wineries on the North Fork have as their most premium wine a meritage blend that includes a good portion of Cabernet. Other wineries produce a Cabernet Sauvignon varietal that is rich and powerful. Cabernet is a full-bodied wine that requires full-bodied food to match its structure. New York strip steak and roast prime rib of beef are two examples.

Roast Prime Rib with Yorkshire Pudding

Ingredients	Amounts
Rib roast of beef (4 or 5 ribs)	about 10 lbs.
Coarse salt and ground black pepper	1 tsp. each
Water	1 cup
Beef broth	1 cup
Red wine	½ cup
Eggs, large	2
Milk	1 cup
Flour	1 cup
Salt	½ tsp.
Reserved beef drippings	¼ cup

Procedure

1. Trim any excess fat from the roast and place in a roasting pan. Rub with the salt and pepper and place in a 425 degree oven for 20 minutes. Reduce the heat to 250 degrees and roast, uncovered, until the internal temperature reaches 120 degrees. (This low-temperature cooking will minimize shrinking and retain juices).

2. Remove the roast from the oven, transfer to a sheet pan, cover with foil and keep warm. Pour off the fat and reserve. Place the roasting pan on the stove and add the water. Bring to a boil, scraping the bits and pieces from the bottom. Strain into a saucepan and add the beef broth and wine. Boil until reduced by half.

3. Heat the oven to 450 degrees. Beat the eggs with the milk and whisk in the flour and salt. Heat a small baking pan in the oven and add ¼ cup of the reserved beef drippings. When hot, pour in the batter and cook for ten minutes, then reduce the heat to 350 degrees and bake until puffy and brown. Cut into squares and serve with the beef. Serve with garlic mashed potatoes and a full-bodied Cabernet Sauvignon. *Serves 6*

New York Strip Steak with Roquefort Butter

Ingredients	Amounts
New York Strip Steak (16 oz. each)	4
Unsalted butter	4 tbsp.
Roquefort (or other blue cheese)	¼ cup
Coarse salt and ground black pepper	½ tsp. each
Olive oil	1 tbsp.

Procedure

1. Soften the butter and blend in the blue cheese with a wooden spoon. Place the softened mixture on a piece of aluminum foil lined with plastic film. Roll it into a cylinder about 2" in diameter and seal off the ends. Refrigerate until firm. At service time, slice off ¼-inch thick rounds and place them on the hot steaks.

2. Place the steaks on a sheet pan and season them with the salt and pepper. Let them come to room temperature before cooking.

3. Rub with the olive oil just before cooking. Cook the steaks on an out-door grill, in a cast iron skillet, or on a grill pan. Start them at high heat and turn them diagonally to get cross-hatched grill marks. If using a chargrill, turn them and put the cover on the grill. Check internal temperature with an instant-read thermometer. For rare, it should read 120 and for medium rare, 130 degrees. Serve the steaks with the Roquefort butter, a baked potato, and a rich Cabernet Sauvignon.
Serves 4

INDEX — PART I

INDEX — PART II